REFLECTIONS
Through the Periscope

My love letter to Dad

JAQUI O'DONOHOE

Copyright © Jaqui O'Donohoe 2021

ISBN 978-0-6451158-0-2

All rights reserved. No part of this book may be reproduced or transmitted in any form or by any means, electronic or mechanical, including photocopying (except under the statutory exceptions provisions of the Australian Copyright Act 1968), recording, scanning or by any information storage and retrieval system without prior permission of the publisher.

Cover design, internal design and copy editing: Lauren Shay – Full Stop Writing, Editing and Design.

For Dad

Contents

Acknowledgements	1
Prologue	5
Chapter One: The end	9
Chapter Two: Always see the light in the dark	19
Chapter Three: Resilience	31
Chapter Four: Overcoming obstacles	45
Chapter Five: Work hard, play hard	53
Chapter Six: Love your body	61
Chapter Seven: Friendship	69
Chapter Eight: There is always enough love to give	81
Chapter Nine: Time is the most important gift	89
Chapter Ten: We all die	97
Chapter Eleven: The power of storytelling	105

CONTENTS

Chapter Twelve: Failure is OK   111

Chapter Thirteen: It's OK to talk about it   117

Chapter Fourteen: Festina lente   125

Chapter Fifteen: Saying goodbye   131

Acknowledgements

I have always known that I wanted to write Dad's story. I was fascinated by the life he had lived, and he inspired me in so many ways. When he died in 2012, I started to collect information from his stories and photographs of his time in the Navy, knowing that one day, I would piece everything together and write his story.

For seven years, I told people I would write Dad's story. Meanwhile, a lot of things happened in my world, and I continued to say to myself and anyone who would still listen that I would write his story "one day".

In 2019, I joined a remarkable group of women called Thriving Women, led by my business coach Emma McQueen. We talked about our goals, and Dad's story was again brought to the surface. I started to think about how his story might look and received plenty of inspiration and ideas from this incredible group of women.

In 2020, the COVID-19 pandemic hit the world, and we were forced in lockdown. I enjoy my solitude and thought I would cope with this change of scenario quite well. Instead, I struggled with the list of things I had said I would always do if I had the time – including writing Dad's story.

ACKNOWLEDGEMENTS

During lockdown, I slowed down for the first time ever. I sat still with my thoughts. I meditated; I relaxed. I realised I didn't want to write Dad's story because if I did, I already would have written it. I wanted to write *my* story – about Dad. I wanted people to know how Dad affected me, how his life inspired me, and how he made me the person I am today. I didn't want to write a factual account of his time in the Navy; I didn't want to write a linear timeline of his life. I wanted people to feel what I felt because of his presence in my life.

So, just like that, I started to write.

And just like that, our story was born.

This book would never have happened without the amazing Emma McQueen and Holly Cardamone (Blue51 Communications). Emma cracked open my self-doubt and ignited my confidence and self-belief and inspired me to believe that I could do anything I set my mind to.

Holly and her wonderful "band of batchers" sparked magic in me, which not only led to the creation of some amazing ideas, but to action and results as well. Holly nurtured me through the process of sometimes getting hard memories out and on paper, giving me the tools and support I needed to make this book happen. She held my hand when I doubted my abilities and gently nudged me when I hesitated. I am so grateful for having her in my life. When I got my story out, she guided me to turn it into a real-life book, which included a fabulous editing girls' weekend away with Ali Drew-Forster.

Without these ladies, I would still be talking about writing this book and never would have started.

Dad's widow, Julie, provided me with boxes of documents and pictures that I spent many afternoons sifting through. Not only has Julie helped me with timelines and stories, but her care for Dad over his final years is something I am forever grateful for.

I must thank the ex-submariners who I reached out to in the Submarine Association Australia Facebook group. Within minutes of asking for assistance, I was contacted by men who had served with Dad and held a huge amount of respect for him. Special thanks to Peter Durrant and Mark Dixon for their assistance. The power of the network is strong, and I know that any of these blokes would drop everything to help me if I needed it. Such is the power of the submarine tribe.

I must thank my amazing husband, Jarrad. His unwavering belief in my ability and support through everything I do ensure I never doubt myself for long.

And Dad. Without him, there would be no story. He is and will forever be my hero.

ACKNOWLEDGEMENTS

This book talks about mental health struggles. If you, or a loved one is struggling please reach out and seek help. The following are some resources that may assist. Don't tackle this alone.

- Lifeline: 13 11 14, Lifeline.org.au
- Defence Force All Hours Support: 1800 628 036
- Beyond Blue: 1300 22 4636, Beyondblue.org.au
- Mensline Australia: 1300 78 99 78, Mensline.org.au
- Open Arms – veterans and families counselling: Openarms.gov.au, 1800 011 046

Prologue

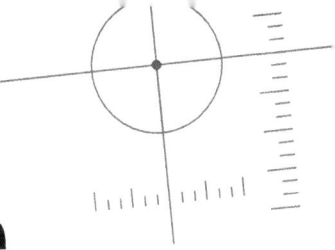

I'm a daddy's girl. Yes, I'm a grown woman, married with a fur baby, and I still refer to myself as "daddy's girl". I always will.

In October 2012, Dad was battling a variety of illnesses. He had been in pain and suffering for over five years, and I had watched his health deteriorate slowly. My life changed rapidly in those five years, as I understood that I wanted to spend more time with Dad while he was still on this planet. Dad was cared for in his final years by the most amazing woman – his wife, Julie. While I assisted her when I could and often spent time with Dad so that she could have a break, her role in his life was such a special one, and her care and love for him were like no other.

Not long after Dad's 59th birthday, I got the call from Julie that Dad was not doing well and the doctor was coming over. This was to be his last night. Julie and I were with him at the end, and we will forever share the bond of that night.

Dad has always been my hero. After travelling aboard the HMAS *Australis* in 1967 from the United Kingdom to Australia as a teenager with his parents and three sisters, he joined the Royal Australian Navy at the age of 16. He travelled the world, usually via the bottom of the ocean in his role as a submariner, which was his passion for many years.

PROLOGUE

He married three times, biologically fathered two children, was a stepfather to five and was a father figure to so many more. He was a proud grandad and beloved friend of many.

Dad's life has always been one I have marvelled at. I live my life based on the simple but strong values he taught me. He instilled in me traits such as resilience, perseverance, and determination, and gave me practical tips for life: the importance of friends, how to see the light in the dark, to work hard but have fun, and that there is always enough love to give.

From the day I watched Dad take his last breath, I have wanted to tell our story. For many years, I told people I would write his book. It took me a long time to realise I didn't want to write a chronological version of his life or simply regurgitate his favourite stories. I wanted to tell my story of how this man inspired me to be who I am today. How eight years after his death, I still talk to him almost daily, and I often refer to his stories. My story may be different from Dad's story, and my challenges and wins may be different, but they have been touched by him in some way along my journey.

Dad was a great storyteller. He loved to read and tell stories. He also loved a good quote and had some beautiful books of quotations that he shared with me and that I still refer to. For this reason, I have shared some of his favourite quotes in this book.

This is my journey of my experiences and treasured memories with Dad. Some people will have different memories and experiences, and they are part of their story to tell.

This book is my love letter to Dad.

CHAPTER ONE

The end

"In this world, nothing can be said to be certain, except death and taxes."
– Benjamin Franklin

I got the call around midday while I was at work. I was sitting at my desk in Subiaco, Western Australia, doing paperwork. My role as a workers' compensation consultant in a global broking firm was busy and hectic. I was always rushing from one place to another. I worked hard, but I had flexibility and loved my job. I was often on the road; I could work remotely from anywhere, and I had a great team around me.

The call came from Julie. "Your dad's not doing well, and the doctor is on her way over." I launched into action. It was not the first time I'd had a call where I had to drop everything and rush to Dad's side. My team knew he was not well, and they knew I had become a pro at managing his ambulance trips to the hospital, often working from his bedside in a hospital room. They were used to me being on the phone, talking Julie through getting Dad off the floor, or sometimes just needing to go downstairs on a Friday afternoon to have a wine in the bar and not talk about it.

CHAPTER ONE

One of my closest friends, Bronwyn, was sitting by me when the call came through. "Just go," she said, and I rushed out.

On my way to Dad's, I was not thinking about him. I was thinking about the work I needed to get done that night and whether I had grabbed my laptop charger – and my laptop. When I arrived at Dad's place, Julie hugged me. The doctor had yet to arrive, and Dad had deteriorated quite a lot.

It had been almost five years since Dad was formally diagnosed with prostate cancer. Although he had formally received the all-clear from cancer, since that diagnosis, he had also developed post-traumatic stress disorder (PTSD), diabetes, mesothelioma, skin conditions from sleeping above diesel engines, and his liver had psoriasis and was failing. His body was basically shutting down.

Dad's room had been set up like a hospital room for almost 12 months. It had that clinical smell about it. Dad had a hospital bed with side barriers, a chair for the shower where his nurse helped him wash, he wore adult diapers, and he could not be left alone at home for fear he would leave dim sims boiling on the stove until they burnt to a crisp – yep, he did that. Or he would get on the roof to "fix something". One time, I came over and found the front door wide open and no one home. I panicked and called Julie, who was babysitting the grandkids. I searched the house and the nearby park, and eventually found Dad walking home from the shops. He was exhausted but alive, and Julie and I realised we could not risk him being on his own anymore. I managed to get some flexibility with work so I could spend more time at their place. Every Tuesday night, I would head over to have dinner

The End

with them both. Julie got some support from the incredible Silverchain nurses, and we were blessed to have gold card status with Veterans' Affairs, which afforded us the ability to care for Dad at home. There was a point when we considered putting him in a home, but Julie and I had looked at nursing homes and welled up in tears at the thought of Dad being there at such a young age. So, Julie took on the role of his full-time carer, and I supported her as much as I could.

When Julie hugged me, I knew this day was different. I felt the tears coming and, despite how strong I had been for five years, I was not ready for this. I went into the backyard and called my boyfriend (now husband), Jarrad, and told him. He offered to come over, but we lived an hour away, so I told him to stay home with the dog, and I would keep him updated. In truth, I did not want him there; I needed to be strong, and I knew I would likely fall into his arms if he were with me.

I shed some tears in the backyard when Julie found me. "I'm not sure I'm ready for this," I told her, as she wrapped me in a big hug.

When the doctor arrived, the tears were forgotten. I kicked into action mode. The doctor said it was time to administer morphine and Julie should not be alone for the night. It was also time for the family to say their goodbyes. We made the call to everyone, and I watched as the doctor and nurse set Dad up. They had a large box that contained the biggest needle I had ever seen – the morphine. The needle was inserted in Dad's arm, and he lay there, restless and confused. I think he knew what was going on and he wasn't ready, either. The box was locked, and the doctor and nurse both had a key so that no one could administer more than the slow drip that started to invade Dad's body.

Within hours, the doctor had left, and the family was over. The grandkids were chasing each other through the house, and I chatted with my brother and sisters-in-law. Julie popped to the shops to get me some clean undies and PJs, and we all had a glass of wine together. The doctor had given us instructions to put drops under Dad's tongue every few hours, and we took turns doing this, ticking it off the sheet when we did. I checked in on Dad often. By now, the morphine was working its way through his body, and he was fighting it. He was restless in his sleep, jerking around and trying to talk to me, but he was incomprehensible. A few of his friends came by and had a chat with him, offering us assistance. About 6pm, Julie and I realised that Dad needed peace. The house was chaotic with so many people there, and we were both in for a long night. We made the call that everyone needed to leave – a hard call to make when loved ones wanted to spend time with Dad, but I believe it was the right one. As soon as everyone left, Dad settled down and started to sleep.

In my time serving as a police officer, I have witnessed death, but not dying. A lot of people will tell you that death can be beautiful. This was not beautiful at all. Dad fought every breath; he did not want to go anywhere. He foamed at the mouth, his body occasionally convulsed, and he would moan. At one stage, I was ready to smash open the locked box with the morphine inside and plunge the whole lot into him just to end his pain. It was many hours before Dad's

The End

body eventually relaxed and he slept, although the foaming at the mouth didn't stop. Julie and I administered his drops, wiped his face, and watched him slowly melt away. We didn't sleep a wink but drank coffee laced with Scotch, watched endless TV, and chatted. It was a surreal night that I will never forget.

In the early hours of the morning, I was snoozing on the couch while Julie tried to sleep in her room. A large bang woke me as the newspaper delivery man threw the paper against the garage door. I opened the front door to a cool, crisp morning. The sun was only just breaking over the horizon, and the world felt still. I sucked in some fresh morning air, picked up the paper, and opened it up as I walked back inside. I laid the paper on the coffee table with the front-page headlines staring at me. I immediately knew that Dad would die that day. The date was the 24th of October. I was born on the 2nd and my little brother, Nic, on the 4th. I felt like this number was speaking to me. The main headline was "Tears for Peter", referring to a young boy who had lost his life in a tragic accident. Dad's name was Peter.

A few hours after reading this seemingly prophetic headline, Julie called me into Dad's room, shouting, "I'm not sure he is breathing!" As I ran into the room, I realised it was the first time Julie and I had been in the room together at the same time since the morphine drip had been inserted into Dad's arm.

Dad sighed, and just like that, he was gone.

CHAPTER ONE

A feeling of peace overcame me. Dad was no longer in pain. The window was open, and despite the sterile nature of his bedroom, I felt the fresh morning air flow through. The lace curtain gently touched the back of my arm, cool and fresh. My immediate and overwhelming feeling was one of gratitude; Dad's suffering was over. My second feeling was guilt; I felt guilty for my gratitude, and it took me a long time to overcome that feeling. While Dad's body continued to move as gasses passed through it, his face was still and peaceful. He was puffy from all the drugs, but his grey hair was soft and full, his eyes closed and still, and his mouth slightly upturned. He looked at peace.

Julie and I had a big hug and shed a tear. Julie called his usual nurse, who was out for her morning walk. She asked us to wait because she wanted to be the one to come over and pronounce him. We were not sure what to do, so we cooked breakfast. I am sure we were both in shock, as Julie scrambled eggs and I made toast. We sat down to a hearty breakfast and started to make a list of who we needed to call and in what order to make sure no one found out via social media. We then realised that the nurse was going to come over and see us sitting there, having breakfast and coffee when poor Dad was not even pronounced dead yet. We quickly cleaned the kitchen, hiding all the evidence of our breakfast. Yes, I am sure we were in shock because I am certain the nurse would not have cared one bit!

The nurse arrived by 8am, pronounced Dad dead and cleaned up the body so that it was ready for the funeral home. All the needles were removed, and his face was cleaned. He looked just like he was sleeping. The funeral home could not

The End

pick Dad up for a few hours and, at first, that concerned me because I knew what happened to a body over time. But in the end, I was incredibly grateful for the delay, as it meant family and friends could come over to say goodbye to him. We had a few visitors pop by early – some were family, and some were Dad's closest friends. All of them brought food. Julie and I didn't have the heart to tell them we had already eaten a full breakfast, so I am sure everyone was concerned we were not eating.

I stood in the kitchen, making a cup of tea for one of Dad's closest mates. I focussed on the boiling water and nothing else. I took a few deep breaths and told myself, *"You will get through this."* I knew it was going to be a rough day. I lost count of how many times I made a cup of tea for one of our guests, but it became my way of escaping the conversation in the living room. I would greet guests, handball them to Julie, then rush into the kitchen to boil the kettle. Each time, I would stand and watch the kettle boil and take a deep breath. *"You've got this,"* I reminded myself.

Seeing people say goodbye to Dad touched my heart in a way that moves me to this day. One of Dad's closest friends sat holding his hand, chatting to him for a while, then came out crying. It tore my heartstrings to see such a strong man have tears in his eyes.

The Navy chaplain came over and performed the "Navy prayer" over Dad's body, and we had a shot of Scotch (except the chaplain, of course). My nephew arrived and asked if he could say goodbye to "Poppy Pete". Julie took him into the room and he walked up to Dad, held his hand, and said,

CHAPTER ONE

"Goodbye, Poppy Pete," just like that. No tears, no drama, just goodbye. I still choke at the memory of it. He was four years old.

Dad was a big lover of collectible cars and trains and had a beautiful cabinet full of old and very antique cars that he loved to show off. He particularly loved the Flying Scotsman steam train and any car that was from *James Bond*. He had ordered a small red London phone box to go with his display, and for weeks, he had been calling the collectibles shop to complain that it had not yet arrived. Dad was getting more and more frustrated and would complain to anyone who listened. About midday, there was a knock on the door. Expecting it to be the funeral home attendees, I opened the door to find Australia Post giving me a package. It was the phone box. I unwrapped it, walked into Dad's room and placed it onto his stomach. "It's finally bloody here!" I told him. Julie and I laughed and left it sitting there on his stomach.

The funeral home attendees arrived at 3pm. We were ready for them by this stage. Julie and I were exhausted from no sleep the night before, and I had lost count of the visitors. I was already sick of flowers being handed to us; as thoughtful as these gestures were, we were running out of vases, and I had incredibly bad hay fever.

We had made endless phone calls all day to advise people that Dad was gone. I finally got through to my big brother, who was on an oil rig in the middle of the WA ocean, and had a beautiful chat with him. He was worried about me, I was concerned about him, and we both had a little cry together. He was getting on the first helicopter out and would be with us soon. My little brother and I had a great chat on the phone, too, and I made sure he was in good company and being cared for. He didn't want to see the body, and I respected that. Calling my aunties was a tough one. My aunty in the UK, Dad's little sister, was in bed when I woke her and told her. "Thank god," she breathed, and I hung onto those words. Yes – thank God. Dad was no longer suffering and no longer in pain. My aunty in New Zealand, Dad's big sister, was off climbing a mountain somewhere, which was not unusual for her, so we left an urgent message for her to be contacted. Other people got a phone call; some were included in a group text. Some conversations were harder than others, and many gave me hope and confidence. All were emotionally exhausting.

The funeral home attendees sought me out with the red phone box in their hand. "What do you want to do with this?" they asked me. Julie responded with, "Can it go with him? He waited so bloody long for it." So, they wrapped it up with Dad's body and it went with him.

When the guests had gone and Julie and I were alone again, I told her I was ready to go home. She, too, wanted to be alone with her emotions. We hugged and agreed to meet the next day at the funeral parlour.

My drive home, which took about an hour, was done in complete disconnect. I could not even recall the route I took. I walked into the house and my fur baby came running to me for cuddles. A fresh bunch of roses sat on the bench, smelling beautiful, and my first thought was relief that my

CHAPTER ONE

man had bought roses because they would not give me hay fever. I looked up and saw Jarrad coming to me with open arms. I collapsed into his arms and broke. I sobbed, and he held me. I could finally let go and be safe. He poured me a strong drink and we sat out the back, looking at the stars, and started to reflect on the life Dad had and what he had taught me.

CHAPTER TWO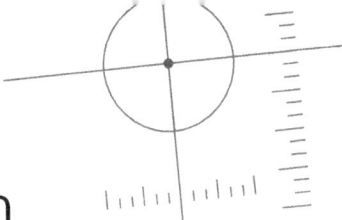

Always see the light in the dark

"It is during our darkest moments that we must focus to see the light."
– Aristotle

For a 16-year-old girl, life is already a mix of hormones and emotions. Add to this the stress of doing tertiary entrance exams in your final year of high school within a toxic, damaging home environment, and things start to snowball.

My parents separated when I was 14. My mother, little brother, Nic, and I moved into a rental home that was close to my school. The house was fine; I still had the luxury of my own room, and my little two-year-old Jack Russell, Devil, lived with us. Devil was not meant to come into the house, but most nights, I snuck her in through the laundry to sleep on my bed and then snuck her back out in the morning. Her cuddles got me through so many nights of tears.

CHAPTER TWO

I struggled during this time of my life as I never had before. I was in a very negative and unhealthy relationship with my mother. As I headed into Year 12, I started to hide away with my friends most Friday and Saturday nights, getting drunk. Not on cheap wine or beer, either – I was buying heavy Jack Daniels bourbon whiskey and drinking a litre a weekend to dull the pain of everything I felt. My mother's influence meant I had unfairly and unjustly blamed myself for my parents' marriage break down. This also meant I blamed myself for the fact that Dad now lived over an hour away in a tiny apartment, which resembled an old box compared to the beautiful home we used to have. In my teenage mind, it was because of me that we did not have that beautiful house anymore, and because of me that I rarely saw my three big brothers.

My parents' relationship was so fraught that Mum would not let Dad in the house, and every conversation was an argument – another thing I blamed myself for. I felt like none of my friends understood what I was going through, and I refused to talk about it if they did try to make sense of it. Dad tried to check in with me often, but I was used to hiding my emotions and being "strong", so I would tell him everything was fine and life was good. But it wasn't.

One morning, I woke to see that my dog had climbed into our blow-up paddling pool overnight and was floating there. She was still alive, so we took her to the vet, but he advised us that Devil had caught parvo disease, and she died later that day. That was the day I hit rock bottom. I had hidden my feelings from everyone in the world, except my dog. She had copped the ugly crying at night while I held her and prayed for the pain to go away, and she licked away the tears and snuggled with me until I fell asleep. She was my rock, and now she was gone. I blamed my mother because she had never arranged any vaccinations for the dog, which only made our relationship more venomous. It was my breaking point.

I took long walks to nowhere in particular. I used to walk across a pedestrian bridge that went over a freeway and watch the traffic flow below me. Four lanes of traffic going about 100km/h became quite soothing to watch. I dreamt of the day I would get my licence and buy a car so I could escape. I had a casual job as a waitress in a Chinese restaurant and was madly saving my money to buy a car.

When you fall down a black hole, there seems to be no end in sight, and nothing and no one seems to be able to help you – particularly when you won't talk about it. Falling into a black hole does not just happen, either. It can creep up on you so slowly that you don't even realise the darkness starting to set in. One day on my walk, I decided I'd had enough. I climbed over the pedestrian footbridge railing and stood looking down at the traffic, holding onto the railing behind me. The adrenalin that went through my body was like a lightning bolt. For the first time, I felt like I finally had some control over my life. It felt like I stood there for an eternity, willing my hands to let go but also chickening out and telling myself I was a failure because I didn't even have the guts to jump. I climbed back over the railing in tears and walked home, internally beating myself up.

The next day, I walked out of home and didn't come back.

CHAPTER TWO

My parents had legally separated when I was 14 years old, but emotionally, it happened well before that. We lived in a beautiful five-bedroom home; a dream home for many families. We had so much space and a big backyard to play in. From the outside looking in, we were the perfect family. However, what many people didn't know was that my parents constantly argued. The accusations and mistrust were endless. I remember being unable to fathom my parents ever loving each other enough to get married, and I still cannot recall one happy memory of my parents together.

Separating would have been hard on both of them – I don't deny that. However, I do recall it being the first time I saw Dad almost break. He had moved about an hour from us to be closer to his work at the Naval base. The first time my little brother and I went to visit, my heart broke for him. From this big, beautiful home we had all shared, he now had a tiny apartment in a complex, with stained carpet and no backyard of his own. His bed was a wooden board sitting atop 12 milk crates, which he had pinched from the local deli, and a mattress on top. His spare bed was my first bed as a child, which he had pulled out of storage and found a new mattress for. His fridge looked like it was the first fridge ever invented, and his couch was falling to bits. However, Dad loved this place. It was his own space and his freedom from what I can only imagine had been a horrible environment for him. We'd lost our house. Mum and Dad had a business together, but their rookie bookkeeping meant they had never paid taxes on the business. Due to the tax office looking for money, they could no longer afford the mortgage, particularly with an 18% interest rate. The bank took the house from them, and Dad was awfully close to declaring bankruptcy.

After the separation, he continued to support us with rent, food and cash to keep us going, but I knew it was to the detriment of his own comfort.

What surprised me the most was the amount of joy I experienced in that dingy little apartment. I still recall our first night. I was given the spare room because my old bed was in it, and Nic had the pull-out couch. We went for a walk when we first arrived to check out this new suburb, and we were pleasantly surprised how close Dad was to the beach. Walking on the beach at night, we joked and laughed and splashed in the water. We had a lot of fun. Dad cooked up a storm for us with spaghetti bolognaise and garlic bread. We ate until we were so full, we thought we would explode. Then came the comedy movies. We watched old *Carry On* films over and over until we cried with laughter and fell into bed, exhausted but so full of love and happiness.

After visiting Dad in his apartment over the years, I now only have memories of joy. We spent endless nights cooking together or walking along the local foreshore to the pub. In summer, we would snorkel at the beach or help Dad's mates scrape the bottom of their yacht clean. We would go to the Navy club on a Friday afternoon and hear stories from Dad and his mates about their days in the Navy, enjoying a sausage in a bun with the other kids there. When Dad had to work during school holidays, he would leave us on the beach at Garden Island, the Naval base where he worked, and give us a walkie talkie and an Esky with food and drinks. He occasionally checked in with us via walkie talkie (this was well before mobile phones), and then he would join us on his lunch break. I am certain this would not be allowed

CHAPTER TWO

in the current day! One time, Dad pulled up to have lunch with us and asked how our morning was going. "There's a snake in the toilet, so we've been peeing in the bush," I told him. He cautiously opened the door to the drop toilet and, sure enough, there was a tail sticking out from behind the toilet. We all stepped back, and Dad threw a stick at it. The "snake" moved, and we realised it was just a huge lizard getting some shade. Breathing a sigh of relief, we went back to our egg-and-salad sandwiches, happy that we could safely use the toilet. Dad was impressed that we had left the snake alone and, over lunch, we talked about what would happen if we were bitten by a snake and the exact steps we should take. This was not unusual conversation for the three of us over lunch. Dad was always teaching us; sometimes practical information, and sometimes what we considered useless information, but it instilled in me a love for learning that has never faded.

Nic and I relished the days where we could play on the beach, read books, snorkel or borrow a canoe. Not only are my memories of the time at Dad's apartment so full of joy, but so are the memories I created with my little brother.

When I was an older and wiser 17 year old, living with Dad in his apartment, I asked him whether he was glad he had found it. He replied, "It might not be the Carlton Ritz, but it's my little place, and I have created many fond memories here, and for that reason, I will always love the place." Despite losing his business, his wife and his family home, Dad managed to create joy and light every day we had together.

Fast forward to 2012, Dad was married to the beautiful Julie and struggling with his health. One of Dad's favourite days of the year was Anzac Day. The day took him on a journey of reflection through his 27 years with the Royal Australian Navy. He would think back to his days aboard the submarines – or, as he would say, "snorting backwards through the Dardanelles" – and the mateship he had shared with so many. It was also a time to reflect on all the friends he had lost: some from accidents, some from old age, and unfortunately, too many from suicide. Dad would proudly put his medals on every year and attend the Anzac Day march. Equally as proud, I would put on his smaller dress medals and attend a dawn service. Sometimes, depending on where we were, I would meet him and his mates at the RSL club for a beer. If I was interstate or couldn't make it, we would share a beer over the phone, and he would remind me of the sacrifices so many had made – and would continue to make – for my way of life.

Dad had three service medals: the Australian Defence Medal with 20-year service clasp, the Defence Force Service Medal, and the Australian Service Medal with Special Ops clasp. He never told me much about his medals or how he got them. Sometimes, I wonder if it was too painful for him to think about. I do know he received one of his Special Ops medals in the post and was not allowed to tell anyone what it was for until 15 years post receipt. Dad told me it was from a trip at sea in 1989 while serving on HMAS *Otama* when I was only four years old. The submarine had been freshly painted, and they were heading to sea to "test" the new paint for eight months. It wasn't until I was much older that I learned some of the things that had occurred on that "paint

CHAPTER TWO

trial", and that Dad had actually been in the East China Sea during the Tiananmen Square incident.

When I asked him about tough trips like this, he would show me pictures of him at sea, swimming with his mates off the submarine deck while someone sat in the conning tower on shark watch. I saw pictures of them dressed up on the deck because someone was crossing the equator for the first time, referred to as a "line-crossing ceremony". There were photos of men sunbaking, sailors crammed into tiny dorm-style beds (each with a smile on their face), and guys smoking in the submarine, which was allowed back then. As a child, I grew up around submarines and often played on board when a sub was in the harbour. When Dad took us on board, Nic and I would look through the periscope, pretend we were blowing up battleships, and chase each other through the hatches. Despite the conditions these guys lived in, I always loved the stories of fun and adventure. As an adult when I asked Dad about his Navy days, he hinted at the emotional toll of his experiences, but he would also remind me that no matter what the adventure, no matter what the story, even if there was death, heartache or loss, there was always joy.

I was always proud of Dad and his mates and grateful for their service – even more so on Anzac Day. During one of my regular Tuesday night dinners with Dad in 2012, I asked him if he would march with his mates at the upcoming Anzac Day service. Dad's faced dropped, and he said, "I don't think so this year," because he knew that physically, he would not be able to march. But he was determined to attend and have a beer with his mates at the RSL afterwards. Dad had been diagnosed with PTSD by this stage and was also struggling to walk unaided. He used a cane, but he would not be able to make the distance of the march. Having your physical abilities hindered can really affect your mental health, and I knew he hated being so immobile. I had a chat with Julie about it, and we put some plans into motion. On Anzac morning, I put on Dad's medals and went to my local dawn service, full of pride as always. It was a stunning morning, and the sunrise was magical. I then headed to Dad's place with my surprise. I had borrowed a wheelchair from a friend's grandmother, and the plan was to push him around the march with his mates. Dad was super excited about it.

Julie had arranged parking for us in Fremantle and, after about 20 attempts, I managed to get the wheelchair open and stay together. It wasn't fancy, but it had wheels and would do the job. What I didn't expect was that half the walk was on grass! We met Dad's mates, and they put us right at the front with the banner. Before we knew it, we were off. My arms had never been so sore in my life as I pushed Dad across the grass and then around the cobbled streets of Fremantle. One of the ex-submariners asked if I was OK a few times, but despite my arms killing me, there was no chance I was handing over the incredibly special task of pushing Dad in that march. I struggled to keep my emotions in check as I watched Dad waving at kids along the street, kids who were yelling, "Thank you for your service," and, "Well done," as we went past. I was so touched by these strangers and incredibly proud of Dad – not only his service but for everything in his life. He was in a lot of pain. Every time I went over a bump, he flinched or groaned, and I told him to shut up because my arms were hurting more! He laughed and told me to toughen up.

CHAPTER TWO

It was a well-earned beer for both of us when we got to the RSL club afterwards. The bar was upstairs and, as we waited for the lift, so many of Dad's mates came up to say hi and tell me how impressed they were that I had managed to "push the old fart" around all morning. Dad's face lit up with every conversation and, as always, he was happy to share a beer with his mates. Dad was exhausted by the end of the day, so it wasn't long before he went home to bed. After dropping him home, I cried the whole way back to my place – not sad tears, but the emotion of the day came to the surface. It remains the most moving Anzac Day I have ever experienced. Despite not being able to march with his mates and not being well, Dad found the light in the dark and shared that light with all of us, making it such a special day for everyone. He would die less than six months later.

Let's wind back to when I was just 16 and ready to throw myself off a freeway overpass into traffic.

I found the light in the dark because I realised that although I was physically in a less-than-optimal environment, my head didn't have to be in that same space. Within a day, I found a granny flat in my friend's yard to live in so that I could continue with school and focus on finishing Year 12. I went to the school nurse, told her everything and asked for her support. She came with me to my house to pack my stuff, and just like that, I was independent. Dad supported me financially while I finished school, and eventually, I moved into his little shoebox of an apartment to live with him, and we created many happy memories together.

Everyone has a different story to tell. Everyone's black hole looks different and is caused by different things. Dad's strength through so much adversity and his ability to always see the bright side of whatever was thrown at him play on my mind every day. I have had plenty of dark moments in my life, but none as scary or serious as that day when I was only 16. I still consider it a turning point in my life, and I am grateful it occurred because it gave me the realisation and strength to do something about a horrible situation. It reminds me that it's OK to ask for help when we are feeling down, and it's normal to have dark days. When we look for and remind ourselves of the light, it makes those dark days more bearable. I now wake up every day looking for the light because it's always there. Sometimes it shines so bright that you relish the warmth of it; other times, it's a tiny light at the end of a passageway that you have to squint to see, but it's always there if you allow your eyes to search.

Thank you, Dad. Thank you for teaching me the importance of seeing the light in the dark. Thank you for helping me realise that it's OK to ask for help. Thank you for supporting me out of my black hole. Thank you for guiding that light towards me when you knew I needed it. Every time I feel myself struggling with the dark, I now ask myself, "Where can I find the light?" And you guide me to it.

CHAPTER THREE

Resilience

"On the other side of a storm is the strength that comes from having navigated through it. Raise your sail and begin."
– Gregory S. Williams

For as long as I can remember, I wanted to be a submariner. As a little girl, I was in awe of Dad and his mates in their sailor outfits. It was instilled in me from a very young age the absolute privilege of serving your country, the sense of duty, and the amazing camaraderie.

Although I was too young to recall the event, I was christened on board a submarine at the wee age of three months, and that submarine is a now a museum in Sydney's Darling Harbour. Now that I live on the east coast of Australia, I am often in Sydney for work, and I love running past HMAS *Onslow*. Dad served on *Onslow* for almost seven years in total and seeing it stirs a deep sense of pride in me. My childhood memories are not of Dad being away at sea, but of him coming back. It's the joy of him returning, of seeing him and his mates in their uniform and hearing the stories of what they did while they were away that I remember most. I am sure some stories were embellished to make them

CHAPTER THREE

sound more exciting, but as a child eager for adventure, they were better than any bedtime story from a book.

I went into high school with everyone asking, "What do you want to be?" I loved the ocean, so my answers ranged from "marine biologist" to "dolphin swimmer" (yep, I'd decided that was a thing). But those I trusted knew I was heading to the Navy – no question. While I had friends in high school who experimented with drugs, I was always the responsible one who stuck to underage drinking instead. There was no way I was going to risk my Navy career over some illegal drugs. It turned out well because I became the responsible person who made sure my friends were safe while they experimented, and I saved a few butts along the way – literally, not just from their parents!

In 1941, women were authorised to enter the Royal Australian Navy, which saw 580 female volunteers enlist in 1942. However, women were not permitted to serve overseas or at sea until 1985 when they could serve on support vessels. Women were not posted on ships; rather, they were only volunteers until the 1990s, and did not serve on submarines until 1998. I was 14 years old when I learnt about women being permitted to serve on submarines, and I felt a stirring of hope deep in my belly that I would one day achieve my dream. I told myself I would be the first female to command a submarine in Australia, and I would go to bed at night with dreams of submarine adventures running through my head. I wore Dad's Navy jumper everywhere, to the point that it fell apart. I studied everything I needed to do and worked out with Dad that I wanted to be a sworn officer, which meant military college – and good grades in

Year 12. It also meant that when I graduated (or what they call "passing out"), Dad would have to salute me, as my rank would be that of a commissioned officer. I had dreams of my passing out ceremony. I would march off the parade ground and Dad would salute me, and we would share a big hug. He made it abundantly clear that although he would be saluting my rank, he would be the more experienced of us! As soon as I was of legal age to apply, I filled out the application form and was ready to go.

I was super excited when I got the letter in 2001, which said I was to attend a day of testing: medical testing, maths and science and psych, and a four-panel interview to see if I was eligible. I studied hard, I quizzed Dad on everything, and I went into it feeling super confident and positive, albeit slightly nervous.

The first test was the psychometric test. I had no issues with English, maths and the like, and the psych test was full on, but I heard Dad on my shoulder telling me to be honest because the truth comes out in these and you cannot beat the test. I finished early and moved onto my panel interview. This was where I believe I shone. We talked about my life experience, my time as an exchange student in the UK and my history of being a Navy brat. We talked about my goals and challenges, and I walked out feeling pumped! Next up: medical. I was 16, fit and healthy, so of course, this bit was going to be easy. I hadn't even given this section a second thought.

Before I even had my shoes off for height and weight, the doctor asked me about my thyroid condition. When I was

CHAPTER THREE

15, I was taken to a specialist because my blood results had come back with a low thyroid. My mother had a low thyroid and noticed some of the symptoms in me, so she had asked the doctor to test me for it. The specialist confirmed that I had Hashimoto's disease, which meant my body could not produce enough thyroxin. Symptoms included tiredness, hair falling out and a slow, lethargic metabolism. Treatment was a small tablet of the lowest dose possible of thyroxin, and I had to take it every day – something I had not even thought about since my diagnosis.

The doctor looked me in the eye and said, "I will have to fail you for your Hashimoto's." I asked him to repeat what he'd said because I didn't understand. He explained that he could not pass me for my medical if I had a condition that required daily medication. If I didn't get my medication every day, eventually (and this could be after many years), I would slip into a coma and die. By signing up to the Navy, there was a very real chance that I would be in a war zone where medication could not be delivered to me, and they could not take that chance. He said I had the right of appeal and I told him I probably would appeal, so he continued with the medical to ensure there were no other issues. Thankfully, there weren't.

I walked out of the building on St Georges Terrace in Perth completely numb. I could not feel my body. Dad picked me up, and I bawled my eyes out. My lifelong dream was going to be shattered over a bloody thyroid condition! I felt numb for weeks after this. Dad helped me get together paperwork and references, which we put to the Ombudsmen to appeal the medical opinion, and then we had to sit back and wait.

Meanwhile, I was working through Year 12, doing subjects that would take me to military college. I suddenly had no desire to complete my studies or to even go to school, but I held out hope that the doctor's decision would be overturned and I would be fine. I pushed on with my schooling with everything crossed that good news would eventually come my way.

It was hard to study when I lived in a little granny flat in my friend's backyard. The flat had a small fridge, kettle, sink and microwave all in one open space. I had a bed, desk and TV and needed nothing more. I had a toilet, and just outside my door was the pool if I felt like a morning dip. I had no shower, so I had to wait until the main house was awake before I could go through the back door to use the bathroom. I always felt like I was intruding when I went into the main house. This beautiful family had taken me in and supported me, yet I just could not open up to them. Instead, I hid in my little flat and drank whiskey and tried to study for school. I relished the weekends when Dad picked me up, and I would spend time with him and feel like I was somewhere I belonged. I counted down the days when I could get my driver's licence, finish school and move in with him. I wish I could have told him how much I was struggling inside.

For months, I dreamt of the Ombudsman's decision being handed down. I finished school and surprised even myself with an excellent tertiary entrance score, which meant I could study anything I wanted at university. I moved in with Dad, got my driver's licence, and started a summer job working at the Naval Base as a trade assistant for a high-pressure air company. I was the only female contractor in a field of about

CHAPTER THREE

500 men, and I spent my days climbing through submarines and ships, getting covered in grease and oil. I loved it! Each day was different, and I enjoyed the fact I could wear my bathers with my overalls over the top, then stop at the beach on the way home for an evening swim to cool off.

One shift, we had to remove a large pipe from the side of a ship. We undid the pipe, and I was on one end while my colleague was on the other, and we were to carry it off the ship. My colleague was a lot taller than I was, and when he stood up, the pipe shifted on an angle, pouring oil all over me from the neck down. The oil went onto the deck and proceeded to spill overboard. This was a huge environmental breach because oil was going into the sea. The Navy was on us rapidly, and the focus quickly went on breaking up the oil slick in the water and cleaning up the oil on the ship's deck. Everyone seemed to forget that I was covered in oil from neck to toe. Once we had cleaned up and had the all-clear from the Navy environmental team, I threw a towel on my front seat and drove home. When Dad opened the back door to our little home, he took one look at me and said, "No way you are coming in here like that," and he shut the door and went back inside. So, there I stood at the back door, effectively in the car park, stripping off my overalls down to my bikini and hosing myself down with the garden hose. I wrapped the towel around me and snuck inside, overhearing Dad on the phone to his mate telling him the whole story of how his daughter ended up with oil from neck to toe. He laughed at me all night and eventually, I saw the funny side. It remains one of my most fun days at work while on the island.

Another fond memory was of being in the "bird box". I was put into a harness and clipped into a small box, similar to what window washers use. I was then hoisted into the air by a crane and hung over the opposite side of the submarine's conning tower. I was suspended about 10 metres in the air, painting the side of the submarine, when a pod of dolphins surfaced below me. I stood there, paintbrush in mid-air, watching these dolphins play around the submarine. It was magical.

On a typical, nothing-special kind of day, I received a letter telling me the Ombudsmen could not override a medical decision, and I would not be joining the Navy. His decision was final. I sat on my bed for a long time re-reading the letter but could not even muster a tear. All I felt was defeat. I felt it in my chest like I had been punched, and deep fatigue set into my bones. It was like everything I had done growing up was all for nothing. I found Dad and showed him the letter. Even worse was the look of defeat on his face. I had wanted so badly to wear the uniform, have him salute me at my passing out ceremony and make him proud. I was robbed of that, and so was he.

Today, I am often called resilient, but I never fully grasped the meaning of the word until I started to write our story. I do know that my resilience was instilled in me by Dad and the way he always picked himself up and sprang back from adversity. Even as a young boy, when Dad left the UK with his family and moved to Australia, travelling on board a ship and docking in Fremantle harbour on the 26th of April 1967, he discovered what it meant to be resilient. Joining the Navy so young and moving away from his family in

CHAPTER THREE

Western Australia to start his Navy career took resilience. When Dad served in the Navy, he was often away from his family, sometimes for months at a time, yet he never complained about it.

As a young girl, I would sometimes sneak into the front family room. This room was just for the "adults", and it was where my parents retired at night to watch TV or host dinner parties. Us kids had our own living area to play in, and we needed permission to enter the front living room because all the valuable keepsakes were in there. I would sneak out of bed regularly as a child, particularly when Dad was home from sea, and he often told me about nights when he would wake to find me standing beside the bed staring at him. Perhaps I was scared he would leave again; perhaps I was just reminding myself he was home. I don't know why, but I am fairly sure it freaked him out a little! When I snuck into the front family room, I would often find Dad lying on the floor next to the stereo with big headphones on. Sometimes he caught the movement, and he would open his eyes and let me lie with him and listen to his music. One of his favourites was Andrew Lloyd Webber, and we would lie there together, listening to the power of that music as it washed over us. I still get emotional when I hear this music. As a child, I never understood why Dad did this; I just figured he liked the music. When I was a young adult living with Dad in his apartment, we talked a little about it. Dad had lost many friends along his journey: some were killed in accidents, some took their own lives, and it always hit him hard because he loved his mates so much. His way of dealing with it and coming back from his grief was music. It taught me the valuable lesson that although we all have resilience to varying degrees, we need self-care to help us through the tough times.

When I realised I was never going to be a submariner, Dad reminded me of the times he had been knocked down by rejection or failure, and how he would lie in the living room, listen to music, and remind himself that it was going to be OK. He left his home in the UK to move to another country, broke his back in the Navy, had two marriages that ended in divorce, had a failed business that resulted in him owing the tax office a lot of money, and he knew he would die with no assets to his name. Yet, he always picked himself up and kept going.

One of my favourite days in primary school was the sports carnival. I was in red faction, and Dad would take the day off to come and cheer me on. He would sit on the sidelines, screaming, "Go, little legs!" as I sprinted past him. Thus, I was dubbed "little legs", and it was one of my favourite things to hear yelled from the sidelines. Fast forward to 2012, Dad was at his worst health wise, and even though I was in denial, I knew he was incredibly sick. As a young boy, Dad had loved cross country running, and he often showed me his trophies and photos of him running. I had started to run in 2011 to cope with the stress of watching his health deteriorate. I wanted to run something for Dad, so I decided that in 2012, I would run a marathon for him to see. I had never been a runner. When I was in the police force, I was always at the back of the pack during PT running sessions, and I have been nicknamed "Cliffy" by my man, in reference to Cliff Young's shuffle because I shuffle rather than run!

CHAPTER THREE

I spent six months training for the Perth Marathon. Despite mornings when I felt tired or sore, I remembered all that Dad had bounced back from, and I would drag myself out of bed. The day of the race was a beautiful day for running. It was slightly cool with clouds casting a shadow. I was so nervous and doubted whether I could finish. I started with excitement in my legs, and it was not long before I was going too fast and had to pull myself back and slow down a bit to make sure I didn't overdo it. My man followed me out on the course, so I was lucky enough to see him a few times. I kept asking, "Have you heard from Dad?" And he would reply, "Not yet – keep going, Cliffy." By the time I reached the 40km mark, I had fought mental fatigue, physical fatigue and the constant battle with my body not to give up. At 41km, I could feel the finish line only 1km away. I came around a bend and saw Dad sitting on a bench with the proudest smile on his face. "Go, little legs!" he screamed at me. I was crying when I crossed the line and hugged him. He looked so sick, yet so proud, and it is a memory I hold dear in my heart. I have since gone on to run more than 25 marathons, as well as ultramarathons up to 100 miles, and every time I struggle, I picture his face as he watched me finish my first marathon. When I am in Perth and I run past that bench along the Swan River, I always get a tear in my eye.

I recall Dad asking me, "What should we do?" when I received the letter confirming I would not be a submariner. "I'm going to travel," I told him. "I am going to get a job, do some hospitality courses, put on a backpack and head off into the world and see what happens." I had not planned this; it just came out there and then. I got excellent grades for school, a testament to some hard work during tough times, and at the last minute, I decided I would use those scores to study forensic science at university. Two weeks into my studies, I was spending more time at the tavern than in lectures. By week three, I was wagging altogether, and in week four, I quit. It was two days after the cut off for the fees, so it was the most expensive four weeks of my life.

I did what I said. I got a job in a children's bookstore, which I loved. I went to night school to get my hospitality courses under my belt and secured a contract working in China for six months as a trainee front office manager in a big hotel. I was pumped and packing for China, completely ignoring the news of some new strain of virus there, when I got the call that the contract was being ripped up because of the risk of SARS (severe acute respiratory syndrome). Another kick to the guts.

I was not going to let this news drag me down for as long as I had with the Navy decision, so I got on the phone to my aunty, who managed some hotels in New Zealand, and I told her I was on my way. I jumped on a one-way flight to Christchurch. My aunty put me on a bus to Queenstown to her friend's place, and a few days later, I started the breakfast shift at the local hotel. For eight months, I had lots of fun, learnt to snowboard, hiked the mountains, did 5am breakfast shifts, babysat for spare cash, and ate my way through Queenstown.

I decided to come back to Australia and surprise Dad for his 50th birthday. The whole family was in on it. I went from the airport in Perth to my aunt's place, and my stepsister

CHAPTER THREE

picked me up on the way home from night shift. I hid in her room until the following morning when we all snuck into the kitchen and made Dad breakfast. By this stage, Dad had moved from his little apartment in Rockingham and was living with Julie and her two children and my little brother, Nic. It was a fabulous house full of love and laughter. As Dad lay in bed, I walked into his room with a tray of pancakes and coffee, singing "happy birthday". He got the shock of his life. We shed some tears, and I knew that I was home, and I was staying.

The loss of the Navy world I had wanted so much continued to haunt me, so I decided I would try for the police force. I entered with the fear that I would have to go through the same ordeal again but hoped that the medical would be fine. I wasn't nervous in the interview, I wasn't worried in the physical, but I was shaky in the medical. I waited a few weeks to find out the result. The week that Dad was due to marry Julie, I found out I was accepted into the police and was given a start date for the academy. It was a magical moment at Dad's wedding in 2004 when I gave a speech and told him what his wedding present was – I was going to be a police officer.

The day I was sworn in and the day I graduated from the academy, I thought about my Navy dream. I'd felt like my world had shattered when I couldn't achieve that dream, but we continue. Dreams get changed, ideas get turned upside down, and life can change in an instant. How we adapt and move with it is what really matters. Yes, it's a horrible feeling, and yes, you can feel downright terrible. But sometimes, we need to remember that maybe it's for a reason and perhaps there is something bigger and better around the corner. Taking things one day at a time and taking it one goal at a time may lead you down a path more different than you ever expected, but perhaps that path is the one you were meant to travel down.

Thank you, Dad. Thank you for showing me that you can fall and get back up. That you can learn to love again. That you can push through those hard times and come out stronger and better for it. Thank you for teaching me I can do anything I put my mind to.

CHAPTER FOUR

Overcoming obstacles

"The tests we face in life's journey are not to reveal our weaknesses but to help us discover our inner strengths. We can only know how strong we are when we strive and thrive beyond the challenges we face."
– Kemi Sogunle

I often think of Dad as a young boy and the courage he had to leave his family and join the Navy. He surprised his family, who all believed he would study horticulture because of his love of gardening as a child. Instead, he joined the Navy.

Enlisted in January 1970, at the age of 16, Dad started his training, with six months at HMAS *Leeuwin* in WA before heading to HMAS *Nirimba* in NSW. He spent just over three years studying at *Nirimba* before being deployed on his first ship, HMAS *Torrens*, in 1973. At *Nirimba*, Dad effectively had to "go back to school". Only this was a school he didn't misbehave in, unlike his previous schools. This school was

CHAPTER FOUR

disciplined and taught him to iron his uniform, march, and make a bed. He loved the discipline, and he instilled that love in me; it is now one of my greatest strengths. In September 1973, when Dad was 19, he graduated from HMAS *Nirimba* and was awarded the technical prize at his passing out ceremony. He even got his photo in the paper. His passing out ball was held at Bowman Hall at Blacktown Civic Centre with 34 fellow graduates. One of those graduates eventually became my godfather.

Dad spent over three years on HMAS *Torrens* and had an eventful time. In 1974, he was on board *Torrens* when they escorted the Royal Yacht *Britannia* for 14 days. Dad stood on the deck in his Navy whites to cheer the Royal Squadron as it sailed into Sydney and *Torrens* continued to escort the Royal Yacht. Members of the Royal household came on board, and a 21-gun salute was fired for Prince Andrew's birthday. Her Majesty the Queen, His Royal Highness the Duke of Edinburgh, Her Royal Highness Princess Anne and Captain Mark Philips attended on the ship, mixing informally with some of the ship's crew. Dad was even photographed chatting with Princess Anne.

Several exercises were carried out on HMAS *Torrens* together with some of the Australian submarine fleet. Somewhere along the course of his time on board *Torrens*, Dad developed a passion for submarines. In 1977, he returned to the UK to participate in submarine specialisation training at the Royal Navy Submarine School in Portsmouth. He earnt his "dolphins" in 1977 on board HMAS *Onslow*. "Dolphins" refers to a badge a submariner wears to signify that he is serving on submarines. It's a huge honour to earn one.

Overcoming obstacles

One of Dad's favourite training courses was submarine escape training. He would get into a very tall swimming pool, enter from the bottom as if coming out of a submarine escape hatch underwater, and swim to the surface in his escape suit. If he held his breath, divers in the water would punch him in the stomach to make him exhale as he ascended to avoid getting "the bends". When I worked with Dad on Garden Island, he took me into the submarine escape training tower, and I found it fascinating. He snuck a few of the escape suits home when we were kids, and we loved to put them on, blow them up and float around the pool like Michelin men.

Dad's report cards from his training days talk about how he "needed to focus" and was "distracted easily". They are almost word for word the same as my early report cards. He knuckled down, though, and you can see a considerable improvement in his maths and engineering skills throughout his training.

In October 1985, Dad severely injured his back while serving on board HMAS *Onslow*. He was taken off the boat and underwent a serious operation at L4-L5 of his spine. I was just a toddler when Dad eventually came home in a full neck brace. He was not allowed to go to sea for a long time and had a long road to recovery ahead of him. He would have struggled with not working, as he loved his job, but the Navy moved him to Harman, the Naval headquarters in Canberra, and he completed his Defence Force Recruiters Course. Dad did not return to a seafaring role on a submarine until he boarded HMAS *Otama* in 1989 as the deputy marine engineering officer. He had a passion for young people and loved his recruitment role. His greatest idea was to get an

CHAPTER FOUR

old inactive torpedo, put it on a trailer, and drive around the Australian Capital Territory and Victoria, visiting schools to talk to students about what it was like in the Navy. Pictures of Dad with school kids sitting on the torpedo were published in various newspapers, which we collected and put into scrapbooks to document his journey around the country. It was a great example of Dad thinking outside the box and coming up with new ideas to engage young people to join the Navy. It was also a great time for us kids because it meant that Dad was home more often.

One particular story I have always loved is the time we all went out for a seafood dinner. Dad was still in a full neck and back brace. He was trying to open a crab claw when he slipped and the claw cut his thumb open. Dad wrapped his thumb in a napkin and rushed to the bathroom. When he removed the napkin and saw all the blood, he fainted and hit his head on the basin on the way down, cutting his head open. After a while and Dad still hadn't come back, Mum went looking for him and found him passed out on the bathroom floor. An ambulance was called to take him to hospital. The paramedics were so concerned about his head and the fact he was in a brace that no one bothered to look at his thumb. When Dad finally came back to reality, he looked at his thumb and said, "What about this?" About four paramedics jumped on his thumb to stop him fainting at the sight of the blood again! I was still in a highchair so cannot recall the actual event, but Dad told me this story so many times, and it was a favourite of mine, reminding me that although shit happens, we can persevere through it. Dad didn't like blood from a young age because when he was five, he fainted while his sister was washing his cut finger, causing him to hit his head on the basin and get a large bruise on his forehead.

Recovering from his back injury took guts and determination, and Dad bore the scars and pain for the rest of his life. However, it did not stop him living life to the full, and he would still carry us kids around, throw us about and return to his Naval duties. Now when I take myself running through the bush for 100km adventures in my trail races, I think of Dad and how he came back from injury. When something starts to hurt, I think about the perseverance and bravery he needed to overcome that injury, and how I never realised the extent of his pain when I was a little girl. It inspires me to push myself harder, but it also reminds me of the importance of caring for my body and making recovery an important part of my training schedule.

One of my toughest ultra races was a 24-hour track race where I ran 800m loops of a running track for 24 hours to see how many kilometres I could run. I wanted to try to run 150km in 24 hours, so I signed up and thought it would be fun. It was torture! Running loops for that amount of time takes you down a mental path that can be dangerous. I sang to myself, listened to some audiobooks, and thought about a lot. I thought about Dad and the life he had lived. I thought about everything he had taught me, and how much his influence continued to play a part in my life. As my feet started to hurt and every step felt like fire on my soles, I turned my thoughts to Dad's illness and how much pain and discomfort he went through in his final years. His back would ache and his feet would swell so badly that he couldn't walk. His head was full of nightmares and scary thoughts,

CHAPTER FOUR

his short-term memory was gone, and his medication would make him hallucinate. His life and death gave me the strength to keep pushing, and I ended up finishing the race in second place with 152km under my belt. As I lay on the grass, crying that it was all over, I sent a quiet "thanks, Dad" to the sky. Another achievement inspired by him.

When Dad got sick with prostate cancer in 2007, his physical ability diminished rapidly. He went from living an active life to struggling to walk to the shops. His determination, however, never wavered. He loved to go to the beach, sit on the sand, and have fish and chips for dinner. When he could no longer walk without the aid of his cane, this became difficult. But he was stubborn, and one night, Julie and I enlisted the help of two of my brothers and we headed to the beach for dinner. We got Dad down to the beach and had a great picnic of fish and chips and cold beers, and enjoyed the sun and sand. As we watched the sky go red and the sun drop, we realised we needed to get Dad back up off the beach. My brothers lifted and Julie and I half carried Dad off the sand until he had stable footing. He loved it.

Dad would still try to do jobs around the house and try to cook and clean, despite being told by us to have a break. I would walk to the shops and find him strolling back with his walking cane, determined to get stuff done, no matter how hard it was. In his later life, Dad had a fabulous collection of walking canes that he loved to show off. His favourite had a handle that unscrewed, and inside the length of the cane was a tube you could store whiskey in.

Dad was adamant that I grew up understanding the power of communication and that it would help me overcome obstacles in life. He believed we should be able to dine with the Queen: speak well, use the appropriate cutlery, start from the outside and work inwards, and do not miss a course! However, he also believed we should be able to eat with our hands at someone's backyard barbecue. It was important to adapt our communication and behaviour to the scenario presented and talk to people from all walks of life at their level, rather than be condescending or rude. This was one of the most important things I ever learned from Dad. My life has literally been in danger – when working as a police officer, when hiking alone, and even while waiting in a restaurant for a friend. At these times, people have scared me, and I have felt in danger. I knew that the way I spoke to people could either diffuse a situation or antagonise it, and this was never more evident to me than during my time as a police officer. The ability to overcome obstacles simply by using the appropriate manner and speech is incredibly powerful.

When I am low, when my body is tired, I remind myself of Dad's strength and determination, and it lights me up. I remind myself of the power of communication. If something starts to feel hard and I want to quit, I remember Dad walking home from the shops that day with his cane, determined to get some goodies to surprise his wife with. I remember his hard work as a teenager, studying to be a submariner because it's what he dreamt of. I remember him coming to Australia on a ship because his family wanted a better life. I remember him teaching me that anything was possible if you had determination and perseverance.

CHAPTER FOUR

Thank you, Dad. Thank you for teaching me that life isn't easy. We all have obstacles to face: some are bigger and tougher than others; some are scarier than others. Thank you for teaching me that the way we respond, react and overcome these obstacles is what's important, and it's what makes the adventure of life so beautiful.

CHAPTER FIVE

Work hard, play hard

*"Don't wait for your ship to come in;
swim out to meet the bastard."*
– Dad's high school graduation card to me

Dad was a hard worker, no doubt about it. His time in the Navy included long stints at sea, and all his mates tell me how hard he worked – sometimes even sleeping in the engine room to make sure things ran smoothly. However, one of Dad's mottos was that life is short and without fun, what's the point? Ironic, given his life was short.

Dad was also extremely patriotic to both his home country of England and his adopted country of Australia. He had a framed photo of the Queen in his living room, and since becoming an Australian citizen on the 17th of August 1982, he proudly flew the Australian flag at his home. He believed that serving your country was an honour, and he was extremely proud to have done so.

CHAPTER FIVE

No matter what situation we would find ourselves in, Dad always had time for fun and a good laugh. He loved a bit of comedy and introduced me and my little brother to *The Goon Show*, an English radio comedy program recorded for the BBC. We had cassette tapes of *The Goons* and would put them on when we went to bed at night and cackle ourselves to sleep.

Dad entered the workforce at the young age of 13 when he got a job selling newspapers for a newsagent in Leederville, WA. In a reference dated 1969, the newsagent owner described Dad as "one of the best" and "most honest and trustworthy". Dad would stand on the street corner and shout, "Get your paper!" as businesspeople drove past. When the traffic light turned red, he would walk along the rows of cars stuck in traffic, selling papers. Dad got very annoyed when the newsagent bought him a new belt that had the coins separated into lines, making it easier for him to give customers change. His old belt with all the money "thrown in" was perfect for getting tips because he would rummage around, looking for change for so long that the lights would turn green and the driver would yell, "Keep the change," as they drove off. This new belt meant Dad could distribute change a lot more quickly and miss out on these bonus "tips". Thus, it wasn't long before he went back to the original belt.

Dad also worked at the Leederville Fish Supply on Oxford Street in Leederville, WA, which was where his love for eating fish and chips wrapped in paper on the beach came from. It was something we did even when he could no longer walk on the sand. Dad kept a reference from the fish shop owner that described him as a "most energetic and very keen worker. He is a very honest and most trustworthy person and possesses a good personality." It was a reference he used to enter the Navy later that year.

Dad had an interesting career in the Navy and was extremely technically minded. He was known as "Chief Tiff", which meant chief petty officer, and his comrades often told me he was the "best chief tiff" they knew. His resume lists technical role after technical role, and he was an expert in marine engineering. Many of his various roles saw him responsible for emergency and routine maintenance, and he could virtually walk anyone through a submarine engine room with his eyes closed.

When Dad left the Navy in 1991, he continued as a Navy reservist. After working at various jobs, he landed a role at the Australian Submarine Corporation (ASC) fixing submarines. This meant that sometimes, he had to follow a sub around the world, which involved long stints away from home. Dad spent a considerable amount of time in Darwin and Hawaii, looking after boats for the war games underway. Although he worked long hours and was often exhausted, he also made time to have some fun. When in Hawaii in 2000, Dad learnt to scuba dive – something he was terrified of doing. He wanted to surprise me (I was an avid diver by then) and take me diving. While he sat on the bottom of the ocean floor in Hawaii, doing the necessary exercises to pass his course, he scooped up a handful of shells that he later gave to a local lady on the beach, and she turned them into a necklace. It was one of the most treasured gifts I ever got from Dad's trips away.

CHAPTER FIVE

Dad came home from his stint in Hawaii with his scuba licence and, a few years later, we managed to go diving together. It was a fun trip down to the south-west of WA to dive on a sunken ship, HMAS *Perth*. We went out with a charter, and the weather was horrid. I threw up over the side of the boat before we even got to the site. We finally got kitted up and down we went to about 20m below the ocean's surface. I looked over at Dad and his eyes told me he was not OK. He looked unwell and was pointing back to the boat. I nodded and watched as he filled his vest with air and started to shoot to the surface. There is a huge risk in ascending from a dive too fast – you can develop air bubbles in your blood that can kill you. It's known as "the bends". I quickly hung off his vest, pulling on the dump valve and releasing all the air in his vest so that we could make a slow ascent. When we got to the boat, Dad climbed on board, threw off his mask, and vomited all over the deck. We never got the opportunity to dive together again.

I recall the night of September 11 in 2001. I was in Year 12. Each Tuesday night, I would stay at a friend's place, sleeping on her living room floor, because we had an early start for our outdoor education class on Wednesday mornings, and her mum would give us both a lift. That Tuesday night, we had watched a movie, and when we turned it off, the news showed footage of two planes hitting the twin towers of the World Trade Center in New York City. It was scary and nothing like anything we had seen before. Dad called me on my mobile to ask if I was watching.

"Yep," I said, dumbfounded. Dad was in Queensland, working on submarines in the port. "Things are a little chaotic here at the moment," he told me. "I may have to go away for a while, but just remember that I love you." I felt like he was saying goodbye, and that scared me.

"Don't you dare set foot on one of those subs and head to sea," I told him. He was still a Navy reservist and I was paranoid he would do anything for his country and would go to sea again. I was terrified of what was around the corner. He wouldn't promise me anything but just reinforced that he loved me, and I spent the night wide awake, thinking about what the world had just turned into. Dad was patriotic and proud to represent and fight for his country; he would readily have jumped on board a sub if he was asked. I am grateful he did not have to again.

There were always fun stories of cocktail parties aboard the submarine in Darling Harbour in Sydney, and stories of onboard celebrations when crossing the equator at sea. When a sailor earns their "dolphins", a big party ensues, the nature of which has shifted since Dad's celebration. You would put your dolphins – a two-inch metal badge with two pins – in the bottom of a yard glass, and your mates would fill the glass with all sorts of alcoholic drinks. You were then expected to scull the drink in one hit and catch the dolphins with your teeth. When Dad told me this story, he added that he went straight to the bathroom and made himself throw up all the booze so he could continue the party and remember the event afterwards! Unsurprisingly, it's a tradition that has since been quashed.

Submarines were a big part of Dad's life; he had a love for those boats. In Fremantle, Western Australia, HMAS *Ovens*

CHAPTER FIVE

was decommissioned and given to the Maritime Museum. Dad worked tirelessly on this boat with my little brother, Nic, fitting it out ready for tourists to come on board and experience the life of a submariner. I know they had lots of fun working on that boat, and Dad loved spending time with his son, sharing his love of boats. Now, when I read reviews from tourists who have been through HMAS *Ovens*, I smile as I think of Dad and Nic and the work they did on board.

Dad's attitude to life taught me so much from a young age. He was always incredibly involved in my schooling and knew most of my teachers on a first-name basis. He wanted to know I was working hard at school and that I was applying myself. He set the example for me that hard work is important, and it pays off. He also set the example that life is short, and we all need to have a little fun along the way; otherwise, what's the point? For me, hard work means meaningful work and giving my all in everything I do. I will set goals, such as run an ultramarathon, and then break them down into small, achievable steps. Then it's about working hard to get the job done. Sometimes, this means having discipline and motivation on days when you just want to stay in bed. Other times, it means working late for a big project you're passionate about or spending your weekends studying textbooks or writing essays. When you work hard to achieve something, it feels that bit sweeter. Then celebrate that hard work!

Dad had a lucky number: 53. It was the year he was born, and it was the number of his first ship deployment. All ships have a number, and HMAS *Torrens* was Dad's first seafaring deployment in 1973. He thought it was a sign of good luck that a big, white 53 was painted on the hull. Whenever we had a raffle ticket or entered a competition, 53 was our number – to the point that I still look for the number 53 today when buying a raffle ticket. However, Dad did not believe in luck. He believed in hard work. And he believed that with hard work, you created your own luck. I am often told I am lucky because I've received promotions, have had the opportunity to move states, been on holidays and have a job that includes travel and corporate entertainment. I don't credit these things to luck – I credit them to the hard work ethos Dad instilled in me.

However, I also believe that if you are not having fun along the way, it's time to make some changes. Fun can be easy to find. It's the practical joke on a work colleague, a night out with friends, a fabulous dinner, or a live football game. It's a surf or a fish or a day at the beach. For some of us, fun is a long run in the bush.

Thank you, Dad. Thank you for teaching me the importance of hard work, the reward of hard work, and the satisfaction it can bring. Thank you for teaching me the importance of celebrating your hard work and enjoying the rewards. Thank you for teaching me how to keep the balance.

CHAPTER SIX

Love your body

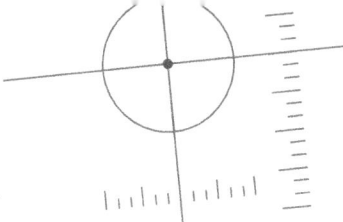

*"You are imperfect, permanently and inevitably flawed.
And you are beautiful."*
– Amy Bloom

I am often asked about my childhood as a girl growing up with four brothers. The question often gets raised, "Were you a tomboy?" Or, "Were you spoilt rotten?" And on occasion, I get, "You poor thing."

I love my brothers immensely, and one of the things I am most grateful for growing up in a house full of boys was the lack of diet culture. From a young age, I had the utmost respect for my body. I didn't always show it respect, such as with the underage bourbon drinking, but I was taught the importance of moving my body and fuelling it with good food.

While the female figures in my life made comments about dieting, tried every fad diet there was, and on occasion even told my young self that I was fat, it was the men in my life who kept me grounded. We climbed trees, played in the dirt and cycled with our friends until the sun went down. At

CHAPTER SIX

night, I would eat pasta and bread and ice-cream and didn't even consider denying myself these amazing foods. We were fit and healthy, and our bodies moved like it.

Cricket was always a passion for Dad. How could it not be? He was born in the UK and migrated to Australia – both countries love their cricket! As a little girl, I was so jealous that the boys got to play cricket and AFL, and I would sit with Dad and watch the Australian Test cricket team every chance I got. I loved the Test matches. Dad would explain all the rules to me, and we discussed tactics. One day, Dad mentioned I should try to play, so we approached the local cricket club and asked if I could join. I was only nine years old and the only female cricket player in the whole district. I became known as "the girl". I had a great team and loved playing so much. I was not the greatest batter, but I was a great bowler and even took a hattrick one day, much to the opposition boys' disgust. My team loved to highlight to the opposition that they had been "bowled by a girl!"

I have such fond memories of Dad teaching me how to bat, bowl and field. We spent hours throwing a cricket ball around. He would also take us to the WACA (West Australian Cricket Ground) every chance he could, and I would play cricket on the grass with my brothers while we watched the local games. I have a very fond memory of playing on the WACA ground at lunch break when the Australian team played. Some of our district was invited to play on the ground, and we got free tickets to watch the game. When I arrived, the usher realised I was "the girl", and I was given my own change room, separate to all the boys. It was a little daunting. I just wanted to be with my team, but I didn't understand how I was so different and how much I was shaking up people's opinions of women playing cricket. I am often asked how it felt to be the only female, but I didn't feel special. I had a great team and played a sport I loved, so being a girl did not come into it for me. I am so grateful that Dad gave me the opportunity to play a sport I loved, despite societal norms.

As I got older, I was told by the district that I could no longer play, as I was too old and needed to join the women's league. I didn't understand it. I was told that as I was "maturing", I couldn't be in the boy's league anymore. It was too "dangerous". I told Dad I would wear a man's box or a breastplate if I had to, but alas, it wasn't allowed. There was no women's league for me to join, so I walked away from playing cricket.

I never walked away from my love of the game, though. Dad and I continued to play backyard cricket, as did my brothers, and I watched the games with him. I loved the one-day format but relished the Test matches. Dad got himself a WACA membership, and we would go to the cricket and sit there for days, enjoying a cold beer and homemade sandwiches. When I was 18 and unsure what the future held for me after being told I couldn't join the Navy, I took Dad's membership and spent five days at the WACA on my own. I had a good book, a packed lunch, and I splashed out (I was broke) on one beer with lunch. I watched Matthew Hayden hit 380 runs against Zimbabwe and take the record for the highest individual run scorer, previously held by Brian Lara. Those five days were so relaxing for me, and I thought so much about what I wanted from life. I walked away from

CHAPTER SIX

that Test match determined that I would apply for the police force. Watching cricket alone gave me clarity.

Dad loved the game so much that he took up cricket umpiring when I was a young girl and was a well-respected umpire in the WA men's first grade. He could spout all the rules, and I enjoyed telling anyone who would listen the 10 ways you could get out in cricket. Sometimes, Dad would take me and my little brother to a game and we would play in the nets while Dad umpired. On one occasion, when we were not with him, we had a call that he was in the hospital. A ball had come towards him at speed, and he had jumped over it but landed on his back. Due to his prior back injury from his Navy days, Dad was taken to hospital for observation but thankfully came out OK. After that day, he was often heckled that he couldn't even jump over a cricket ball, let alone throw one.

After Dad got sick and his health deteriorated, he didn't go to the WACA as much. One of my favourite players, Adam Gilchrist, was playing his last game in WA, and I wanted to take Dad. I drove us in so that he didn't have to worry about crowds on public transport, and set him up at his seat, ensuring he was comfortable. A common symptom of PTSD is the inability to be in or manage large crowds. Thanks to his PTSD, Dad struggled with any crowd, and I knew how uncomfortable he must have felt. He didn't last the day and we left early, but it was beautiful to have that last day at the cricket together, and I relish that memory.

After Dad's death, cricket continued to be a love for me and my husband, and we both love to attend big games at the MCG, particularly on Boxing Day. One afternoon, as we walked to our new local RSL club, we noticed a sign advertising for women to join the local women's league. It brought back memories of the fun I had playing when I was younger, so I emailed the club to see if I could come down. I went to a training session feeling nervous about what I might find. I found an amazing bunch of ladies who shared my love of playing cricket and wanted to have some fun. I was hooked. I put my hand up to be their wicket keeper and fell in love with this role. The first game we played, I walked out and soaked up the sunshine, sucking in the smell of the freshly cut grass, and I could feel Dad with me, cheering me on. I could literally feel his pride and it made me smile.

I find cricket exhilarating and relaxing all at the same time. Being the wicket keeper means I am involved in every ball. When the bowler runs in, I have to watch that pink ball in their hands like my life depends on it, and when the bowlers are fast, sometimes I think my life does depend on it! Hearing the ball thud into my gloves when I take a catch is the best feeling, and seeing a teammate take out the middle stump while I duck as the ball and bails fly towards my face gives me a sense of pride and joy. You cannot stress about work or life when you are concentrating on a pink ball flying at your face. We are a group of ladies who support each other, lift each other up, and have fun along the way. I have made some incredible friends. In my second season, I joined the committee, and I see a long future for my love of cricket. Every time I walk onto the field, I think of Dad and the love we shared for the game. I thank him for letting me experience that love when I was younger, when it wasn't socially acceptable for girls to play. He never let me believe

CHAPTER SIX

I had any limitations because I was born a female; instead, he inspired me to break down those barriers and do what I wanted, regardless of my gender.

Dad was never still for long when he was young. Stories of his long-distance running always filled me with joy. He trained in boots, which would strengthen his calves and ankles because of the weight, and then run the event barefoot because he would be faster. He also loved riding horses across the moors and had a strong love of animals and nature. Although I have not adopted his tactic of wearing boots to train or running barefoot, I often think of his stories and running medals, which I still have on display, and take inspiration from them. For every marathon and ultramarathon I have run, Dad has been there in the back of my mind, cheering me on and offering practical advice, such as, "You're dizzy, drink something."

My first ultramarathon was the 6 Inch in Western Australia – 45km in about 45 degrees Celsius. We started at 4am, and I am sure the temperature was already above 30C. I felt so good until about the 35km mark when I began to feel dizzy and nauseous. I woke up lying in the bush off the track. It appeared I had fainted and rolled down an embankment. As I sat there, ready to cry, I saw green tree frogs jumping over my legs – most definitely a hallucination. I screamed to the sky, "Come on, Dad, I really need you right now!" I got up, dusted myself off, and shuffled the last 10km to the finish line, where I called Jarrad and burst into tears. "I think I almost died," I sobbed to him. But by the time I got home and had a glass of champagne to celebrate, I was already planning the next race. When I undertake my ultramarathons and I'm running through the night, and it's dark and cold and I am hurting all over, I will often look to the sky and say, "Give me some strength, Dad." He always does.

Dad carried some horrific scars on his lower back from his back operation in 1985. He often told me he got those ones for free – why would you pay for scars? It was ironic that a man in the Navy had a hatred of tattoos. He also reminded me of the body's ability to heal.

Dad was not always kind to his body, particularly his liver. Growing up in the era Dad did, the answer to all one's problems was a beer with your mates or a Scotch in the dark at home. When you lived in a metal tube under the ocean's surface and had traumatic experiences, you were taught to drown them, not talk about them. In Dad's later life, he often had nightmares. He drank heavily, mainly to get to sleep. Unfortunately, I followed his footsteps for far too long in this regard, and from far too early an age. Although Dad and I haven't always respected our bodies, I have learned so much from his experience. I am now proud to say I have a huge amount of respect for my body and try to pass that message on, particularly to young women, every chance I get.

Before I could even join the police force, I had to obtain my Bronze Medallion in swimming. I can swim comfortably, but I am not a naturally strong swimmer. I will never forget the nights when I towed Dad and Julie the length of the pool at home, practicing my rescue moves. It was hard work for me to get this medallion, particularly when the two guys sitting the exam with me were massive and I had to tow them

CHAPTER SIX

50m while they only had to pull me. I also had to undergo a fitness test that involved sit-ups, push-ups, strength testing and a beep test. The first time I attempted this, I did the sit-up wrong, failed the whole test and had to re-sit it. I sat in the car and cried afterwards. When I got home and told Dad, he had me on the floor every morning, correcting my technique to get it right. Sure enough, I aced it the second time.

Thank you, Dad. Thank you for teaching me that my body was made to move and grow. Thank you for teaching me the importance of looking after it, nurturing it, and respecting it. Thank you for telling me I was beautiful and telling me often so that now when I look in the mirror, I see my beautiful blond hair, my big brown eyes, my strong body and my smile. I haven't always looked in the mirror and seen beauty, but when I do, I see your eyes looking back at me and remind myself how important it is to love your body. Your body failed you in your final days, and mine will one day, too, but I plan to get as much out of it before that day comes. Thank you for teaching me how.

CHAPTER SEVEN

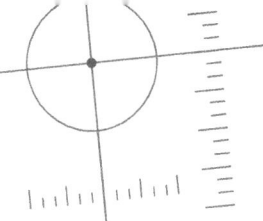

Friendship

"It's the friends we meet along the way who help us appreciate the journey."
– Sarah Boddy

My last year of high school was tough. I had moved out of home, drank heavily, and tried to study for my tertiary entrance exams. I struggled with my emotions and hid inside myself more than ever. I had great friends at high school, who often asked me how I was going, and I believe they were genuinely worried about me. Yet I continued to push them away. I could not wait to get out of school, run from everyone and pretend I didn't need anyone. I was sure I would be fine on my own. I was an introvert by nature, I loved reading, and I felt like I just did not want to waste my energy on anyone else. Boy, was I was wrong!

After I left Year 12 and cut off a lot of my friends from my world, it was Dad who reminded me of the fun times I'd had with my friends. Some of his stories made me see the light again and realise the importance of friendship.

CHAPTER SEVEN

Dad had met Julie while I was in high school. We often spent weekends at her place. My new stepsister and stepbrother were of a similar age but had a vastly different life to mine. They were social and had friends over all the time and were always having fun. Initially, I was extremely uncomfortable in this environment and wasn't sure how to act. On Saturday nights, a large group of people would come over, ranging from Dad and Julie's mates to young kids playing video games with my brothers. It was a sea of activity and energy. I wanted to be swept up in it all, and sometimes I allowed myself to be. However, I felt awkward with so much energy and fun when I was struggling inside. One particular night, I watched as Dad took the car keys from some of the guys who had been drinking and offered them a place to crash or a taxi fare, and I started to realise the importance of having a good friend.

Growing up, I heard plenty of stories about Dad and his mates, and they were always entertaining. In his younger days, Dad had a school friend called Monkey. He and Monkey would steal bread from the school canteen and generally get up to schoolboy mischief. The boys went to boarding school together and played marbles; it was said that was where Dad learnt his selling and "conning" skills. If Dad was having a bad day and didn't want to go to class, he would munch on orange peel because this would raise his temperature and matron would send him to bed. It was also said that Monkey and Dad would steal cigarettes and get caught smoking in the bushes or their bedroom; however, Dad always attested to his children that he was never a smoker! Dad also had a love of horses. Every year, he would go along with his big sister pony trekking on Dartmoor. He cared for the ponies

Friendship

with his sister in winter and they spent time riding in the woods, playing cowboys and Indians with war paint, feathers and fake guns.

When Dad progressed into the Navy, his friends became his life. While I was never sure of most of his friends' real names, I grew up with many uncles and aunts – such as Uncle Bubbles, Uncle Frizzy and Uncle Sheepdog. I was blessed to have Dad's friends in my life. Before Dad's mother moved back to the UK from Western Australia, she often had young guys appear on her doorstep, asking for a place to crash for the night. Most were sailors who were in town and just needed a bed. She had a rule that anyone who appeared on her doorstep must know both Dad's middles names before she would let them in. The number of sailors who surprisingly knew this information was staggering, but she always gave them a feed and a bed. This did not stop even after she moved back to the UK, with many visitors who knew Dad arriving on her doorstep for a cuppa.

When I was 10 years old and still grasping the importance of friends, I found Dad sitting in the living room one night, listening to his favourite Andrew Lloyd Webber tunes. We talked about my friends and how much I enjoyed playing with them. I told him I wanted to have a party, just because. My birthday parties up to that age, and for many years after, were co-parties with my little brother because our birthdays were two days apart. But I just wanted to have a party with my mates and celebrate our friendship. Dad said he would think about it. The following morning, he pulled out an encyclopedia and told me about the Boston Tea Party. This was a protest that occurred in Boston in 1773, involving

CHAPTER SEVEN

a group of American colonists who dumped chests of tea received by the British into the harbour in protest of taxation. Not something overly exciting for a bunch of 10-year-old girls; however, Dad's rule was that I could have a party if we all learned something along the way. Thus, my Boston Tea Party was formed. Five of my closet girlfriends frocked up in their best dresses and came to my place. We used the Royal Doulton China, ate sandwiches and cupcakes, and had our photos taken in the garden. It is one of my happiest memories with my childhood friends, and I loved the connection we shared, even at such a young age.

Dad's friends often visited when we were young, and they were always offered a meal and a bed. As a kid, we were so blessed to hear some of their stories. We were told tales of adventure, including cycling around lochs in Scotland and going from pub to pub along the way to stay warm, and cocktail parties on board submarines in Sydney Harbour. One particular sailor was over from America and had brought with him a doll's house. Dad had purchased it in Hawaii and somehow talked this sailor, who was sailing to Fremantle on an aircraft carrier, to lug it with him on his voyage. When he arrived in Fremantle, Dad had him over for dinner as a thank you. I thought this sailor was some kind of Father Christmas, bringing a doll's house with him! That doll's house sat at the end of my bed for many years and brought me a lot of joy.

I was heavily involved in the Scouts as a child, as was the whole family. At the age of 14, I decided I wanted to do an exchange program and started to save my dollars. Fundraising became my life for 12 months. Every Saturday morning, we set up the barbecue out the front of Bunnings. Dad knew the manager and thought it would be a good idea – now, it's an Aussie tradition. We would sell chocolates and raffle tickets, and Dad hosted a quiz night for me. Eventually, I saved up all the money I needed and headed to the UK to stay with another Scouting family that lived in Stoke-on-Trent. I was 15 years old when I boarded a plane on my own to head off on this adventure. I hadn't had the greatest year, with the pressure of school and my deteriorating relationship with my mother taking their toll. I wrote Dad a letter that I gave to him at the airport as I said goodbye.

Dad,

Since before I was a teenager, I have dreamed of this day. Not only a day where I can prove I can be self-reliable, I can break away from all the surroundings that do continue to depress me. This, I believe, has been the best year of my life. I say that even though I started it with the worst ever New Year, and continued that with one of my most hated holidays. Came home to move house and have you move away, not to mention losing another friend, Laura. I then lost some of my school friends, including my best. But, through all that, it's been my best year. I now live in an area I like being in. I have made new friends and moved up the social ladder at school. I now have friends who care, and I have a social life. But, best of all I believe I have really matured. Not only matured but learnt. This is the first time I have felt myself get older. And now I'm off to make friends from places you grew up. I couldn't be happier, as John Stuart Mill once said:

"Ask yourself whether you are happy, and you cease to be so."

CHAPTER SEVEN

This trip means more to me than anything at the moment. I need to get away, to feel independence and freedom.

This note is to let you know how much I appreciate your work, time, and effort. Not to mention your love. You've never doubted me, and you have helped me reach this goal. For that, I say THANK YOU.

Love, Jaq

This trip was life changing for me. I stayed with a beautiful family, the Machins – John, Karen and their three children – who taught me so much, and I had so much fun with them. We travelled to places in the UK they had not even been to, just so I could see them. I'd always wanted to go to Scotland and visit Loch Ness, so they packed up the car and we went. I wanted to see the house Dad was born and grew up in, so they drove me to Wolverhampton and I stood in front of his old house, which still had the same old wooden front door. They even drove me to see my aunties and Grandma in Gloucestershire. Since this trip, I have remained best friends with John and Karen, and I love them and their beautiful children – and now grandchildren – dearly. I was proud to have them witness us when I got married.

I stayed with the Machins for two months, including Christmas and New Year. The day I was due to go home, we were up super early for the two-hour trip to Heathrow Airport. We all piled into the back of John's work van with my suitcase and beanbags – there were no actual chairs for us. As we sat on the M6 motorway, going slower than I could walk, I started to worry about getting on the plane. Sure enough, we missed it. I called Dad and he said, "Shouldn't you be on a plane?" I replied, "Well, I can see the plane – it's taking off right now!" We laughed it off as another adventure, and I headed into London with the Machins to spend another 24 hours with them before I could get my next flight. As I had missed my original flight, I had no flight attendant to accompany me on the plane the next day, which meant I had to travel completely alone. Dad talked me through what I needed to do in customs and gave me some safety tips. John and Karen hugged me goodbye, and then I had the freedom of being in an airport on my own. I loved the responsibility and adventure. I found lifetime friends in the Machin family, and I am incredibly grateful I had the opportunity.

In Dad's later years, I was over for dinner one night with him and Julie, and he mentioned that he would like to have a party for his 60th birthday.

"But you're about to turn 59," I told him.

"Yeah, but I might not make it to 60," was Dad's reply.

The fact this was very much reality hit me like a punch to the stomach. But in my true form, I hid it well. "You're not getting a 60th until you turn 60," I told him defiantly. "However, there's no harm in having a 59th." Julie reached out to a heap of Dad's old friends and asked them if they would like to come to a small barbecue for Dad's birthday. There was no mention of, "It might be his last birthday," or, "We might not get the chance for his 60th." But I have a feeling some of his close friends knew this was the case. A heap of ex-submariners, who I had called "uncle" growing

CHAPTER SEVEN

up, responded, and we started planning for a Sunday afternoon of fun on the 21st of October 2012.

My hubby couldn't join me for the day because he was playing in a lawn bowls competition, so I headed down to Dad's place on the day. It was about a 45-minute drive. On the way, I got a call from Julie, telling me that her daughter, April, who was expecting twins in 12 weeks, was being induced and was on her way to the hospital. Could I get everyone organised for the barbecue and host the event? "Sure thing," I said, and called my little brother, Nic, to get his butt over and help me out. Julie's sister was dropping off some salads for us and we had some snacks, and I figured since these ex-Navy boys used to eat their meals in a metal tube below the ocean, they wouldn't be fussy.

Dad was super excited when we got there and could not wait for his mates to arrive. We moved his big armchair to the backyard, as it was a beautiful day, and Nic and I prepped everything we needed with the magic of Julie's sister's truckload of salads. Dad's friends arrived, including my godfather from South Australia, who had flown in to see Dad. I recall standing at the barbecue with Nic and looking over at Dad, who was in his element. His mates were feeding him and getting him beers from the fridge. They were telling stories about old times together and sharing a laugh about their adventures.

They shared stories of their children and grandkids, and the pride on their faces was beautiful to witness. I felt like I was a part of something really special. While I cleaned up beer bottles and took away plates, I had a real feeling of love for these men, who were making Dad feel so special and loved when he was obviously in a lot of pain and struggling with the knowledge he might not make it to 60. The men themselves were absolutely charming; they even washed up for us as I cracked jokes about how many submariners it took to do the dishes. As we finished lunch, we heard the wonderful news that April had given birth to twin boys, and we all had a toast for these two beautiful babies, who, although born prematurely, were doing great. As I held my glass in the air during the toast, I realised Dad's life was so full and so big that it was going to take the birth of two boys to make up for his life ending. I still held hope that Dad had years in him, but reality continued to punch me in the gut, and I knew deep down as I went through photo albums with him that afternoon that I was not only collecting stories but also picking out his favourite pictures to use at his funeral.

After a few hours, Dad was exhausted. I was a little worried about getting him to bed. Dad was wearing adult nappies by this stage, and I didn't want him to feel embarrassed in front of his mates if I made him go to bed. Seeing two men I had grown up loving and admiring help Dad off to bed made my heart soar. I grew up believing men were strong and never meant to show emotion or cry. At the time, I myself thought that showing emotion was weak, which was why I used humour every time I wanted to burst into tears about a situation Dad was in. Here were two of the toughest guys I knew, teasing and laughing with Dad as they carted him off to bed, and Dad was laughing along with them. I was reminded that day of the importance of friendship and the importance of seeing the light. We all knew Dad did not have long left. And we all knew that Dad knew he did not

CHAPTER SEVEN

have long to go. This was likely going to be the last time this band of mates would be together, but instead of being sad about it, instead of wallowing in sorrow, they laughed, joked, bantered and told stories as if they were at any old barbecue at a mate's place. The joy I felt for this group of men that day will never leave me. They taught me the power of friendship, humour and knowing that no matter how dark it gets, there is always light. I drove home that night exhausted. Physically, I was stuffed; emotionally, I was a wreck, but I felt such joy.

Three days later, I was called to Dad's bedside to help Julie monitor him while he was administered morphine via a drip. He died the following morning. As I looked through the photos I had earmarked for his funeral and we discussed the plan for his farewell, I realised that the stubborn git had got his wish. He had just held his own wake four days earlier with all his mates. He might not have reached the age of 60, but he got the birthday party he wanted.

Eventually, Dad did get his 60th party. On his actual 60th birthday, Jarrad and I joined Julie and Nic at the Naval Club in Rockingham with a group of Dad's mates to celebrate what would have been his birthday. We stayed in a shack on the beach a short walk away and spent the day sharing stories, eating birthday cake, and toasting the memory of Dad. The Navy Club presented us with a plaque they erected on a propeller that sits out the front of the club. My favourite line on the plaque reads, "Sailor, rest your oar." It was a beautiful afternoon. We walked back to the shack along the beach before we were hit by a large storm, which shook the shack all night as we played Scrabble and drank Scotch. Dad would have loved it.

Friendship

Many years after finishing school, I rediscovered the importance of having a good network of friends, and I regretted the time in my life when I cut off so many beautiful friends because of my inner demons. By that stage, I'd had a solid friend for many years who lived in another state, I had some good social friends, and I was in a strong relationship. Jarrad and I had decided to move states for my career, knowing no one and scared about what would happen. Having to start from scratch and make friends all over again was a scary concept, and I was certain I did not want to only make friends in a work environment. I embraced all of Dad's stories about the importance of friendship and putting yourself out there. So, I started to attend Rotary meetings, book clubs and running events to meet people. I joined a cricket club and began to connect with similar people – people who shared my values and brought joy into my life – and we discovered beautiful friends at Jarrad's new bowling club. It was more important than ever that we had a good group of friends who could support us, cheer us on, and hold us accountable. I was fortunate that by putting myself out there in our new city, I made some incredible friends.

Dad's funeral was full to the point that even standing room was taken. I will never forget standing at the front of the room to give his eulogy, looking around to the sea of faces in front of me, and realising that friends are the family we choose. They are the reason we find the light in the dark, and they are the joy in our lives. I nurture my friendships now and treasure them, and I am grateful that Dad taught me the importance of a good friend.

CHAPTER SEVEN

Thank you, Dad. Thank you for teaching me the importance of having friends in my life. Thank you for teaching me to open up to my friends and not be afraid to share my story with them. Thank you for teaching me the importance of being able to "lie in the gutter and look up at the stars with a homeless man, and also to throw on your heels and have dinner with the Queen." The ability to talk to people from all walks of life and make such diverse friends has given me relationships I will forever cherish. Thank you for teaching me the importance of friendship in my marriage. Thank you for being my friend.

CHAPTER EIGHT

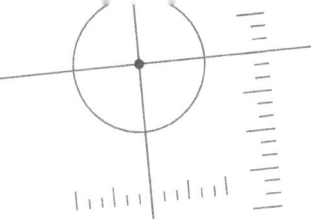

There is always enough love to give

"Being deeply loved by someone gives you strength, while loving someone deeply gives you courage."
– Lao Tzu

I still remember losing my first dog, Devil, as if it were yesterday. I was 16 years old and going through my toughest year yet. I was trying to complete Year 12 tertiary subjects and I was in a highly toxic environment at home, which caused me to spiral down a very dark hole. Devil was my absolute life saver during those dark times.

One morning, Devil was sick. It turned out she had parvovirus, and she died later that day. I was devastated; I had loved her so very much, and it broke my heart that she was gone. I had lost the ability to find comfort in a cuddle with my dog at night, I had lost the ability to find solace crying into her fur, and I had lost the only living thing in the world I could open up to, talk to and be honest with.

CHAPTER EIGHT

Many years later, I had the opportunity to get another dog. My brother's dog had puppies, and I had helped care for the poor runt of the litter because he was not feeding well. My brother offered him to me, and I said, "Yes!" I named this little ball of fluff Mak, and I asked myself, "How could I love another dog like I had loved Devil?" It quickly became clear to me that you do not run out of love to give. There is no set amount; it's an endless supply. You always have enough love to give.

When Dad was still healthy and loving life, living with his new girlfriend Julie and his kids were young adults, he travelled to the UK to see his sister for her birthday. Dad had so much love for his sisters. The whole family came together to celebrate, and he spent weeks holidaying with them and having fun. One of my favourite stories of that holiday was when the family was travelling on a canal boat through the English canals. Dad's beautiful nephew cracked a joke at Dad's expense, so Dad picked him up and threw him into the canal! His sister looked up at him and said, "Did you just throw my son in the canal?"

"Yep," Dad replied.

"Very good," she said, before they all fished Dad's nephew out of the water and back onto the boat.

The night before he was due to come home from the UK, Dad was chasing his niece down the stairs when his foot caught the corner of the stairwell and he cut it open. Blood poured all over my aunt's carpet. Dad's foot blew up to twice its size, but he still managed to get on the plane the next day.

He hobbled onto the plane and made sure the air steward was aware he was injured. Thus, he was treated like royalty, with the steward at his beck and call, bringing him Scotch and whatever else he needed for the long-haul flight.

When Dad arrived home, he was greeted at the airport by Julie. He hobbled off the plane straight into her arms and proposed. I was living in New Zealand at the time, and I remember bawling when he called me with the news. I also felt so proud. This man just never stopped loving. Julie was to be his third wife, and he loved her so much. He loved her family so much. Despite his past heartache and loss, he never stopped loving, and I wondered how he could find so much love within him.

When my little ball of fluff came into my life, I started to understand where Dad found all this love. It is this bucket of infinity that we have within us.

When I was a little girl, Dad would tuck me into bed and say, "I love you to the moon and back." One night, I asked him how far away the moon was, and he replied, "Basically, it's infinity," which got my little brain confused. So, I asked, "What's infinity?" And he replied, "How much I love you." Thus began my little comeback to his "I love you to the moon and back" comment every night. "I love you to the moon and back times infinity," I would say. And as he turned off my light and closed my door, Dad would whisper, "Plus one."

Dad's wedding day to Julie was a celebration of so much love. He got married on the naval base at Garden Island in WA. A busload of guests, who had all been security cleared and

CHAPTER EIGHT

given a "wedding pass", pulled onto the causeway in front of my car. My car carried the bride and the bridesmaids, and we were not yet even dressed. I told the security guy on the gate that I had the bride, so he needed to hold up the bus to give us a bit more time to get ready. The poor guests had no idea that the reason why they had to have their identification checked again – and why the bomb mirrors were being slid under the bus – was because of us. We rushed to the senior sailors' mess where we had room to get ready, and quickly threw on our dresses and makeup before we made our way to the beautiful, sunny courtyard.

It was the perfect day. I walked down the aisle as a bridesmaid and caught my little brother's eye first. He was the best man, and we both looked at each other and smiled, knowing how proud we both were of Dad on this special day. My next glance was at Dad, and the love and joy on his face made my heart swell. I was overcome with the emotion of seeing him, waiting for his bride with so much happiness. With the sun shining on a very warm April day, and the ocean in the background blue and sparkling, Dad said his vows to Julie. I was a proud bridesmaid and my cheeks hurt at the end of the day from smiling so much. The room was full of friends and family, and we laughed and danced well into the night, celebrating their love.

Dad's love bucket never ran empty, especially when his grandkids came into this world. He loved seeing the kids and would often get on the floor and let them climb all over him or play with them in the pool. Their laughter brought him so much joy. I began to understand what love meant when I watched Dad in his later years; the emotions, behaviours, warmth, and respect you could have for another person. It can be scary to open your heart to someone else; you can end up hurt, and you can end up lonely. Watching Dad put himself out there after so much pain and watching him become whole and open to experiencing love taught me so much. I learned from him that it is scarier not to live a life with love than to avoid love because you might get hurt.

Seven years after Dad's death, and almost 15 years since I had met Jarrad, I walked down the aisle. I had grown up scared of marriage after seeing two people, my parents, end up hating each other so much. I could never understand how my parents could have loved each other so much that they married and had children, only to become so bitter and have so much animosity towards each other at the end. For that reason, I was determined to never get married. For many years, Jarrad and I talked about getting married, and I always found a reason to put it off. We knew that if we were going to do it, it would be small and simple. I often considered getting married when Dad was sick. I knew he wanted to walk me down the aisle more than anything in the world, but I refused to get married just to satisfy that wish. I wanted to make sure I was doing it for the right reasons. Later in Dad's illness, I knew I had left it too late because he would not physically cope with the day. I do not regret my decision because I know that Dad was with us on the day in spirit, and my little brother, Nic, stepped in on Dad's behalf, which would have made Dad so proud. It made me proud.

Our wedding was planned while slightly drunk in Thailand with friends. Our friends were going to come to Melbourne from the UK the following year, and we decided we wanted

CHAPTER EIGHT

them to be our witnesses if we got married. As Jarrad and I smoked a cigar and had a beer on the balcony of our hotel room, we decided we would ask them that night if they would be our witnesses when they came to Melbourne, and we would work out the rest later.

The day came about quickly. The ceremony was small and simple, with only family and a handful of friends. It was perfect. I stayed the night in an apartment around the corner from the registry office with Karen, my witness, and I was filled with joy and love, not apprehension and fear. I woke early in the morning, sat on the balcony and chatted with Dad's angel. I admitted to him that I was a little scared. I was scared about committing to marriage, and I was scared I might get hurt one day, but I was also filled with love and joy. I didn't hear his response, but I felt it. *"I love you to the moon and back times infinity, plus one."*

You will always have enough love to give, so never stop giving it, and never stop being open to receiving it. While many will experience pain after love, that does not make your bucket dry up. Your love bucket never runs dry. Whether it's a flutter in your stomach when you see your soul mate, a private smile or giggle when you share an inside joke, loving a child so much you just want to watch them sleep, a beaming smile or laughing fit that hurts your stomach when you spend a weekend with your girlfriends, or sharing your hopes and dreams with someone – your love is a never-ending supply.

Thank you, Dad, for teaching me about love. Thank you for teaching me the importance of having love in my life. Thank you for teaching me that we all deserve love and respect.

There is always enough love to give

Thank you for teaching me that even if your heart gets broken, even if there is pain and suffering along the way, it's important to be open to love. Thank you for teaching me never to stop loving. Thank you for teaching me what real love looks like. Thank you for loving me.

CHAPTER NINE

Time is the most important gift

"The trouble is you think you have time."
– Buddha

Growing up, I did not want for much. I am sure I always asked for things – what child doesn't? I didn't "want" for much, though. We always had a comfortable home. I always received Easter eggs from the Easter Bunny and Christmas presents from Santa. I was spoilt on my birthdays and even the Tooth Fairy looked after me with the odd 50¢ coin. What I always wanted was time. Time with Dad was treasured because he was often away at sea, and it taught me the importance of time together. We cannot replace it, and we cannot buy more. Time is short, and none of us lives forever. When you give your time to someone, you give them the greatest gift of all.

One of my absolute fondest memories of spending time with Dad was when I was a young girl of about 10 years old.

CHAPTER NINE

Dad, my little brother, Nic, and I packed a backpack each and walked to the local Scout hall. We were all members of the Scouting community, and it played a big part in our lives. However, we didn't walk down the street; we bush bashed through the wetlands surrounding the lake and came out the back of the Scout hall, where there was a campsite with a fire pit. We set up a tarpaulin over a tree and one on the ground and laid out some sleeping bags. We started a fire and sat around it sharing stories. Dad then called the local pizza shop and asked them to drive 400m down a certain street, where they would be greeted by flashing lights and someone to collect the pizza. Nic and I hid in the bush until we saw the pizza car slowly crawling down the street, the driver likely worried about what was to come. We jumped out of the bush with torches with red and green filters on them and waved them in the air. Dad watched from the bush as we paid the driver and then slunk back into the bush. I still laugh at what this poor driver must have been thinking that night! After a night of pizza and toasting marshmallows on the fire, we cuddled up in our sleeping bags and slept under the stars. It was a magic night and that precious time spent together is a favourite memory I hold dear to my heart.

Dad would often take us on camping trips. One of our favourite places to go was Peaceful Bay Caravan Park, which was run by Dad's friend, Uncle Bubbles. The caravan park was on the beach, and we would spend our time swimming in the ocean, hiking, building fires, and wearing ourselves out. My love of the bush and camping undeniably come from these childhood trips, and now, I love nothing more than disappearing into the bush for a run or a solo multi-day hike.

Peaceful Bay was where Dad started to teach me how to drive. I was about 14 years old, well under the legal age to drive, but it was also not the first time I'd been behind the wheel. From as young as I can remember, I would sit on Dad's lap in quiet neighbourhood streets, steering the car while he worked the pedals. I could not wait to learn how to drive, so Dad started teaching me young in a controlled, safe environment. By the time I did my driver's test at 17, I had been driving for years and passed easily.

When I was 16, Dad and I had bought a car for about $800. It was a bomb. It was a white Ford Falcon with no front windscreen and no front seat. We used a milk crate as the front seat, just so we could get the car around the corner to Dad's apartment and move it around the car bays. Whenever I stayed with Dad during Year 12, and later when I moved in with him after graduating, we spent every spare moment working on my car. I thought she was the most beautiful thing in the world, and I would wash her every week with tenderness and love. We replaced the brake cable and put in a new windscreen, which was incredibly difficult. We installed an old car seat we had found at the wreckers. I saved my money, buying one tyre at a time until I had four, and was surprised with a spare tyre for my birthday. Dad made me change my own brake pads and tyres so many times that I could do it on my own almost blindfolded. He was adamant I was not going to drive on my own until I could manage my vehicle, which meant being able to look after myself if I was stranded on the side of the road. Not only am I so grateful that he ensured I was self-sufficient with my vehicle, but I also loved the time we spent together working on my car. It was often late at night under the light of a

CHAPTER NINE

torch or the patio bulb, trying to be quiet and not wake the neighbours.

I moved in with Dad for a short time when I was 17. We shared his small apartment for about six months, and although it wasn't the most glamorous place to live, and we only had the basics to survive, we had so much fun living together. Our nights were spent eating home-cooked meals, such as spaghetti bolognaise or chilli mussels, and on occasion, we would walk to the pub together. Dad loved to cook up a curry over a few days and would share containers with friends, telling them they would need to use refrigerated cotton buds to wipe their butts because it was so spicy. We shared a laugh over comedies and we shared books. We even joined a touch rugby team with Dad's workmates. I found this ironic because it was Dad's idea, yet he broke a rib in our first game, which meant he never played again. Meanwhile, I ran around on a Friday night with his work colleagues while he watched and laughed from the sidelines with a cold beer!

It was the second time he blamed me for breaking his rib. The first time was when he took me and Nic jet skiing and I drove with Dad sitting behind me. I tried to be clever and throw him off, and I succeeded. The problem was that I threw him off with such force, the clip of Dad's life jacket was in the perfect spot to connect with his left rib as he hit the water at speed, thus breaking the rib! He tried to do something a little calmer following that, so we hired a small catamaran and sailed in the bay near home. Unfortunately, the owner hadn't put the bungs in, and after a while, we realised we were sinking and waved to people on the beach to get the rescue boat to come to get us. We were towed back in and given our money back – which we took to the pub and had lunch.

We didn't have a lot of money, we didn't have a lot of things, but we had time together, and it was a part of my life that I am incredibly grateful for.

On numerous occasions, Dad and I had to "save" each other from the neighbour by pretending there was a phone call. Our beautiful neighbour was about 90 years old and lived alone. If she caught you outside, she would chat for hours, so we started taking our mobiles with us whenever we hung the washing, then we would call each other when necessary so that we didn't get stuck for hours. She was such a lovely neighbour, though, and we loved her dearly.

Dad's duplex apartment was badly run down. It shared walls with two other duplex apartments. The front and back yards were also shared, and the apartment had a small kitchen and bathroom with two bedrooms. There was no laundry, so Dad had a washing machine in the bathroom, and he had to build a board over his gas cooker for bench space. I loved this little apartment so much, though, and I have such fond memories of staying there. Each time I think of that home, I get a smile on my face remembering the fun we had together there.

I am so grateful that Dad taught me the importance of time. I am a terrible gift giver and often forget to arrange gifts, but I will always make time for those I love. My beautiful nephew lives in Tasmania, and for his 10th birthday, I sent him football tickets for him to watch his beloved Hawks play in Launceston. As he sat in his seat, he looked next to

CHAPTER NINE

him and there I was, sitting with Jarrad. The reaction on his face was the best present ever for me. Time spent with those you love can never be beaten.

When I joined the police force in 2004, I was a baby-faced 19-year-old with aspirations to be a cop forever. I wanted to work my way up the ranks and achieve everything I possibly could as a police officer. I had big goals, and I worked hard. I was in a plain-clothes investigator role within 12 months and had undertaken my sexual assault and child interviewing course. I knew I wanted to be a detective and work with children and victims of abuse. Then Dad got sick. I continued working as a cop for some time after he became ill. I was not sure how sick he really was, and I was confident he would get better. He was then diagnosed with PTSD from his time in the Navy and started to have nightmares and hallucinations. He dreamt I was shot at work, and I would get calls from him at strange times of the day and night, asking if I was safe. I worked long hours doing shift work, and I was not spending enough time with Dad. I knew from my childhood that time was more important than anything, so I made a tough decision. I resigned.

I didn't have another job to go, and it was a scary and stressful time in my life. But I wanted to be able to spend more time with Dad while I still had him. It was particularly difficult because I knew how proud Dad was of me as a police officer. He would tell random strangers all the time that his daughter was a police officer and would introduce me to people as "my daughter, the cop". I was so scared that by resigning, Dad would not be proud of me anymore. One night, we had Dad and Julie over for dinner, and I told him I was going to resign but that I was also worried he would not be proud of me anymore. Dad looked at me with a tear in his eye and said, "I will always be proud of you, my daughter." I knew then that I was making the right decision. I told myself I would go back to the police force when Dad was better. We got five years with Dad before he died, and from the day I resigned, I spent more time with him. Regular dinner dates and weekends, as well as Christmases and Easters together, created the most beautiful memories. I found another job in the insurance industry, and it turned out I found my niche and have loved my career ever since. It was an easy decision for me in the end because I listened to my heart for what I needed most.

Time is still my most valued commodity. If you get my time, it is because I value you. If you give me your time, I will treasure it accordingly. We cannot escape the ticking clock, and we all get the same minutes in a day, so choose how you use your time wisely. You will never get it back.

Thank you, Dad. Thank you for all those moments we shared. Thank you for the nights we cooked together, the nights we worked on my car together, and the nights we camped together. Thank you for the drinks we shared, the memories we made, and the laughs we had. Thank you for always making time for us. I only wish we still had time.

CHAPTER TEN

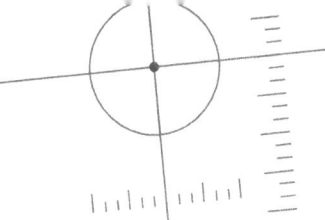

We all die

"There is no passion to be found playing small – in settling for a life that is less than the one you are capable of living."
– Nelson Mandela

It should be obvious by now that Dad loved his quotes, and it's a love I have inherited, too. One of Dad's favourite one-liners was, "Two things in this world are certain: death and taxes." It is still one of my favourites because it's so true. It has led me to understand and acknowledge that we all die, and it's how we live that really matters.

The first experience I can recall of death was my grandad's passing in March 1997. I was 12 years old and at a Scout camp on Rottnest Island. Mum was there, too, because she was one of the Scout leaders. We got a call from Dad that his father was very sick and unlikely to last the next 24 hours, so he needed to get to Melbourne ASAP. Mum was standing at the payphone and turned around and said, "Grandad is really sick." I turned and walked back to my friends. I knew how serious it was. I could tell by the tone of her voice, and I could tell they were planning their flights to Melbourne. I sat with my friends, who were talking about lunch, but I could not

CHAPTER TEN

hear anything they were saying. I had no understanding of death and had never experienced it before. I felt numb. I was not incredibly close to my grandad because he lived on the other side of the country; however, I loved him dearly and had such fond memories of him. My most recent memory of him at the time was when he and Nanna Clark flew in for Dad's 40th birthday to surprise him, and we danced at Dad's party together, laughing the whole time.

Mum and I headed home from Rottnest, and on the ferry ride back to Perth, I wrote a short poem. I gave it to Dad and asked him to read it to Grandad at his funeral. Dad hugged me and asked if I would like to read it instead. At first, I was super excited that I got to go to Melbourne with Mum and Dad for the trip, but then I realised Dad was giving me my first experience of death and a funeral, and this was a big deal. It felt very grown up for a 12-year-old. I reflect on that trip, and I am so incredibly grateful that Dad took me along. I stood in front of a group of mourners and read my poem bravely. I still recall the poem off by heart:

> *You've lived life and you've lived it well*
> *But now's the time it's all gone wrong*
> *It's time to say goodbye, forever till I die*
> *And as we lay you down to rest*
> *We'll never forget how you always did your best.*

Later, I sat in the back of the room at the wake with my uncle, who asked me how I was. I loved my uncle from the first time I could remember meeting him, when Dad told me Uncle Neil was coming to visit. Uncle Neil was in the Royal Australian Air Force (RAAF). He was Dad's stepbrother because his father had remarried to the most beautiful soul, Celia. I could not remember Uncle Neil, so I asked Dad what he looked like. He replied, "Well he is missing some fingers from a dog bite, and he only has half an ear." I was shocked! When we picked up Uncle Neil from the airport, I was even more shocked to see that all his fingers and ears were intact. Dad had got me again with his prank jokes. I told Uncle Neil about this and we still joke about it, even more so now because he has since lost part of one of his fingers from a saw blade. Perhaps Dad's joke was a jinx.

I was not so much sad at Grandad's funeral as I was in awe. The room was full of people who loved my grandad and had experienced some of his 81 years of life. Some were sad, some shared stories and jokes, and I was so grateful to be able to witness such a celebration of someone's life. Death did not scare me, and I suddenly appreciated it on a whole other scale. I realised that a group of people would be standing at my funeral one day, and I wanted to give them something to celebrate. Deep stuff for a mere 12 year old.

Many years later, I attended the funeral of Grandad's wife, Celia. I called her Nanna Clark, and she was one of the most beautiful souls I had ever met. Grandad and Grandma, affectionately referred to as M, had divorced, and M had since moved back to the UK. Grandad met Celia in September 1975 and later married her on a 41-degree day with Dad as his best man. Dad immediately gained four stepbrothers: Mark, Gary, Neil and Glenn. Dad was close with Uncle Neil, likely because of their military connection. Neil and his wife, Sally, both served in the RAAF, and Dad loved to visit them and their beautiful children. Celia had the amazing

CHAPTER TEN

ability to bring people together: she never forgot a birthday, always sent a Christmas card, and loved her family so much. She developed emphysema and died in 2013. I managed to visit her while in Melbourne shortly before she died, and I shared photos with her of Dad's funeral, Dad's wedding and her great grandchildren. We chatted about the family for a long time, and she held me in a beautiful hug before I left. She made a big impact on Dad's life for the love and comfort she gave his father, and I know Dad loved them both dearly.

Dad would tell me about his friends who had passed away, but they were always the facts and not the emotion. Still, I am grateful he shared those stories. One of his closest mates died while driving around Australia with his wife on their motorbike. It was a bucket list moment for them, but a car went into the wrong lane, and just like that, it was over. A friend died suddenly from a heart attack; another was killed in a fire. These stories made me realise the fragility of life and how quickly it can be taken away. I started to really understand that life is short, and it is so important to live each day.

When Dad's mother returned to the UK from Australia, she lived with Dad's sister until her death in 2006 at the age of 88. Grandma had lived a full life. She had lost her first husband, a spitfire pilot in World War II, before marrying Dad's father, Basil, and having four children. In 1966, the family was in the tourism trade in Cornwall and decided to pack up and move to Australia to escape the crippling industry. In Australia, M started an antique business in Perth before returning to the UK and living in Pewsey,

Wiltshire, with my Aunty Jo. Aunty Jo was M's carer in her later years and did an incredible job. Dad was in the UK to celebrate the 50th birthday of his youngest sister, my Aunty Tosh, when M died on the night that Dad was due to come home, delaying his departure. I know he was grateful to see his mother one last time before she died and speak at her funeral, as he'd had a very close relationship with her. I didn't attend the funeral, but I was touched to be able to spread her ashes when I visited the UK later that year. With my two cousins, who were close to M, and Aunty Jo, who had cared for her until the end, we took Grandma's ashes, spread them in a nearby river and had a toast to her beautiful life. It was incredibly special to have this moment and remember a lady who had been larger than life.

Dad told us he had prostate cancer on Boxing Day in 2007. We'd had a great Christmas Day. The Machins were over from the UK, and Jarrad and I had camped in the living room after a big day of eating, drinking and partying with the family. The next morning, we were just about to head home after a breakfast of left-over ham when Dad said he needed to tell me something. "I had some tests done recently, and I have prostate cancer," he said with a chuckle.

The chuckle confused me. "Are you joking?" I asked him.

"No," he said, more serious this time. "I'm having an operation in a few weeks to remove the prostate."

I was in total shock. I drove home, confused. We spent the afternoon at our friend's house for a big barbecue, and I ended up sneaking into their living room, lying on the couch

CHAPTER TEN

and trying to comprehend what was happening. I didn't understand if this was serious, and I didn't understand how serious it was.

We were back at Dad's place for New Year's Eve and had a Scrabble championship between all the family. It was lots of fun, and there was plenty of eating and drinking. At midnight, we all jumped in the pool to celebrate. I looked over at Dad a few times and caught him sitting back, just watching everyone. I could tell he was scared he might not survive the surgery. I knew the risks were small, but I, too, was scared. On the day of his surgery, I experienced a complete lack of appetite for the first time in my life. I literally could not stomach eating my dinner until I had the call or message that he was OK. The hours and minutes dragged on, and it felt like it was taking forever to get the news. Finally, about 7pm, we had the news from Julie that Dad was in recovery and all was well.

Dad came home with a catheter but otherwise seemed to recover well from the operation. However, the downward spiral into ill health had started. He was home a lot more with time off work, and his PTSD came to the surface, causing nightmares, hallucinations and excessive drinking. His body was starting to fail on him, and I saw him rapidly go from a fit middle-aged man to an extremely sick old man.

Over the next five years, Dad got worse and was no longer stable on his feet. He had a walking cane and often had falls that resulted in him in the emergency department at Fremantle Hospital. I am sure Julie knew some of the ambulance officers by name, they were called out so often!

One particular year, I got the call on Boxing Day that Dad had taken a tumble and was taken by ambulance to the emergency room. When I arrived, I found him in his bed, angry with everyone because he was going through withdrawal symptoms from the lack of alcohol. The doctor told Julie and me that he likely only had another six to 12 months left in him. I said I was going to get a coffee and clear my head, and walked through the sterile, clinical hospital corridor to the lift and pushed the down button. The doors opened, and there was my little brother standing in the lift, looking exactly like Dad did at his age. The resemblance was uncanny, and I burst into tears. As Nic wrapped me in a bear hug, I sobbed. I knew death was inevitable for all of us, but I hated knowing it was coming closer for Dad.

Whether Dad had 12 months to live or more, it was important he got to live life until the end rather than wallow in the sadness that it might be over more quickly than we had hoped. This was part of the reason why I loved Julie for taking on the responsibility of caring for him at home. She gave him so much love to ensure his last few years were about quality rather than quantity, and gave him the privilege to die at home instead of in a hospital bed.

We all die. We cannot escape it. We can try to prolong it, we can avoid it and refuse to talk about it, but it will get us all at the end of the day. Dad taught me this from a young age, and I have accepted it. When I go running or hiking alone in the bush, I am often asked by people, "Aren't you scared?" and, "What if something happens and you die?" I always respond with, "Well, you have to die of something."

CHAPTER TEN

My hubby knows full well that if I die out in the bush, it will happen while I'm doing something I love. I would rather take a chance, put myself out into the world and have some adventure and fun than play it safe.

Thank you, Dad. Thank you for teaching me about death. Thank you for teaching me that dying is completely natural. Thank you for making me unafraid of death and, thus, not afraid to live a life of adventure. Thank you for making me appreciate the beautiful thing that is life. We all die. That's the truth.

CHAPTER ELEVEN

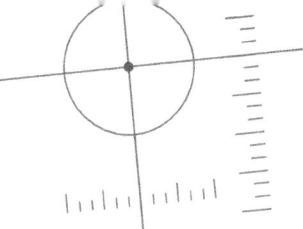

The power of storytelling

"Never let the truth get in the way of a good story."
– Dad

Dad was a storyteller. There was no need for storybooks at bedtime when I was a little girl because he would tell the most entertaining stories. As kids, we often asked him if his stories were real. He would grin and reply, "You should never let the truth get in the way of a good story." As such, I have grown up to love reading and telling my own stories.

From his childhood days in the UK, Dad would tell me about his mischievous ways with his friend, "Monkey". They would run across the shale, which would start to move once they were on it. Dad would always run faster than Monkey because it meant the shale would move for Monkey and cause him to lose his footing and fall over. On occasion, they would sneak into the church near their boarding school and steal some food. The young boys were always up to

CHAPTER ELEVEN

mischief, and Dad was often getting into trouble. He loved his childhood, however, and often told me about riding his horse across the moors and playing with his sisters.

One of my favourite – and most horrifying – stories of Dad's was when he was at boarding school. There was a kid who bullied Dad, and Dad really did not like him. I am not sure to what extent the bullying was, but Dad decided to stand up for himself. He hid around the corner with an English stinging nettle and when the kid came around the corner, Dad hit him across the face with this stinging nettle. What Dad didn't know, however, was that the kid was allergic to stinging nettles. He was rushed to hospital, and Dad was given the cane. He was so mad he was given the cane that when the kid came back to school, Dad did it again! This time, he was expelled. It is actually a rather shocking story, but when Dad told it, with his arms swinging and his face lit up in horror that he got the cane, you couldn't help but laugh at him.

One of Dad's favourite lines was, "Don't tell me what to do." He loved to say this to supermarket operators who told him to "have a nice day", or to waiters who told him to "enjoy his meal". He always got a kick out of the expression on their faces when he replied with this line. It got him into some trouble in America, however, when he was working in Hawaii. He was at a bar, and the bartender poured him a Guinness and told him to have a nice day. Dad responded with, "Don't tell me what to do." The bartender reached under the bar, pulled out a shotgun, pointed it at Dad and said, "What did you say?" Dad quickly retreated, trying to explain it was a joke. It still did not stop him using the line.

The power of storytelling

As I've mentioned, after Dad's health deteriorated and he was diagnosed with PTSD, he started to have nightmares. One was a recurring nightmare where he was looking through a periscope while under the water in a submarine. Through the periscope, he was trying to navigate the submarine through two giant propellers of an oil tanker. The idea was to come up under the propellers and then "hide" under the oil tanker so that the sub could not be detected on sonar. Dad rarely told me stories like this of his Navy days – most of his stories were about fun, laughter and crazy adventures. To get a rare glimpse of the scary world he must have lived in while in a tube under the ocean gave me so much respect for the job he did, and the job many continue to do.

I understood Dad made some scary calls in his time as a chief petty officer, and he had experienced some very scary moments. You only had to see him waking from a nightmare to know that life in the Navy was not all fun and laughter for him. He also enjoyed telling us stories of when the submarine would surface, and everyone would jump into the ocean to cool off, particularly when crossing the equator when he would sit in shark watch in the conning tower. I loved hearing these stories and seeing photos of him on his beloved subs. It looked and sounded like such an adventure, which was part of the reason why I grew up longing to be a part of that world.

After Dad left the Navy and worked for the Australian Submarine Corporation, he travelled to various cities around the world, following the fleet of submarines to "fix them up" while in port. Once he was in Exmouth, WA, working on the naval pier for a few months, and brought the family up

CHAPTER ELEVEN

to spend a week with him. I was only about 12 years old, and while we were up there, Australian model Elle Macpherson was also there, shooting commercials for a tourism campaign. It was off season, so it was noticeably quiet, and poor Elle had to listen to us kids screaming and running around the pool while she and her crew tried to relax in the hotel. I loved that we got to share some time with Dad while he worked up there. We had to leave in rather a hurry, however, when a cyclone came bearing down on us. We flew out in horrible conditions in the smallest plane I had ever been on, and it was incredibly scary. Uncle Bubbles sat in front of me and he cracked jokes the whole take-off to keep us calm.

Dad often sent me pictures of his trips away. When he worked in Darwin, he sent me photos of stunning sunsets and emus that would come to his apartment door, looking for food. Dad explained that he had to get in a small dinghy to get out to the submarine in the harbour and time the tides – which came in and out of the harbour quickly – for boarding to ensure he did not get stuck. I asked him if there were crocodiles in the water and he told me his mate was climbing up the rope ladder on the side of the boat at high tide, and a crocodile jumped up and snapped at him, which made him climb up a lot quicker! I am sure this story was embellished, but I loved it anyway. Life was one big adventure for Dad, and it is a motto I carry with me still.

As much as Dad loved telling stories, he also loved to hear a good story. One of his favourites was *The Phantom of the Opera*. Dad introduced me to this musical when I was quite young. We would watch the movie, sing the music, and talk about how we would go see the performance live when it finally came to Perth. When it did come to Perth, Dad was working in Darwin and could not go with me. I was so upset, but Dad bought me a ticket and, at the age of 15, I sat in the crowd on my own and was taken on the Phantom's journey, mesmerised by the beauty of the theatre. After Dad's health declined and he barely left the house anymore, it was announced that *The Phantom* would be coming to Perth again. I bought tickets and ensured Dad got a seat that did not require him to walk upstairs and did not have anyone next to him, as he struggled in a crowd. I knew the length of the show would be a struggle for him, but we both went along and were mesmerised by the show once again. I knew this was a big day for Dad. He was uncomfortable in crowds, and it was a big effort for him to be out of the house that long. Towards the end of the show, I realised I had achieved my girlhood dream of seeing *The Phantom* live with Dad. I felt so much gratitude for that moment.

I learnt so much from Dad's stories – most importantly, you can entertain anyone with a good tale. You can also turn anything into a story. As a child, I always had my head in a book, and as an adult, I wish I had more time to have my head in a book. When Dad told a story, you were hooked from the start; he could grab your attention, hold it, and have you laughing and crying. I like to think I have adopted some of his skills, and I enjoy telling people my stories.

This book is my story, which is my experience with Dad. Some will have a different story, and that's OK. We all have our own story to tell, and we should enjoy telling it. Don't forget to share your stories.

CHAPTER ELEVEN

Thank you, Dad. Thank you for the absolute joy your stories brought to my life. Thank you for the laughter that worked its way out of me just when I needed it. Thank you for passing your love of storytelling on to me. Thank you for teaching me how to appreciate a good story, how to tell a good story, and how to listen to a good story. I hope our story continues to be told.

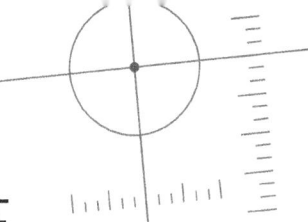

CHAPTER TWELVE

Failure is OK

"The best way to guarantee a loss is to quit."
– Morgan Freeman

In 2017, I embarked on an epic adventure. I had a backpack carrying about 20kg and was hiking 1000km self-supported on the Bibbulmun Track in WA, from Kalamunda to Albany. Most people do this hike in three months. I was planning to do it in 28 days. I was pushing out 10–12-hour days of walking and I LOVED it. I relished being alone in the bush with just my thoughts and doing simple things like putting up my tent each night, cooking my dinner and fetching water. I was right in my element.

On the second day, a blister appeared from nowhere on my foot. It didn't hurt, so I just taped it and kept going. By day 10, my foot was so heavily infected, the doctor told me I would lose my foot if I continued. I was only 350km into my hike, and my hubby made the call to pull me out. I had given him the power to pull me from any crazy adventure if he needed to, and I would not fight it. By not fight it, I mean there were tears and I was fighting it, but I finally listened and stopped.

CHAPTER TWELVE

The next few days, I fell down a black hole. I had to visit the doctor daily for dressing changes, and I was on heavy antibiotics. I felt sick, and I felt like a failure. I cried myself to sleep most nights. I had trained for this adventure and planned it for about 18 months, and I felt like I had let everyone down. Some people reminded me that it was "just a hike", but I felt like I would never come out of this black hole.

When I could finally put a shoe on, I travelled down to Albany, which would have been the finish line, and met some girlfriends down there. While I spent the nights at the pub with the girls, I spent the days on my own, walking on the beach or the Bib Track, making peace with myself. The trip ended on Anzac Day when we did a dawn service together before having breakfast. It was one of the most moving dawn services I had ever done. Albany did the service beautifully, including a red flare as a sign of respect to the boats that left its port so many years ago, carrying troops on their way to the battlefields of World War II. My mindset that day also helped me realise the importance of living each day to the full. I felt like a failure, but I was reminded that failing was part of life, and we needed to learn from it and push on.

After breakfast, I left the girls and went to climb Bluff Knoll, WA's tallest peak, on my own. It was tough because I was still struggling to wear a shoe, thanks to my blister, and my foot hurt but I pushed on to the summit, where I sat and had a good old chat with Dad's angel. Anzac Day holds so many fond memories for me: attending marches and dawn services with Dad, hearing his stories over beers at the RSL. After Dad's last Anzac Day in 2012, Nic and I marched in

2014 to celebrate 100 years of submarines in Dad's honour. It was a proud moment for both of us, and we cherished being able to march beside Dad's comrades. Three years later, attending Anzac Day in Albany after my failed hike was also special because I reflected on Dad's "failures" and how he bounced back from them.

Dad had married Julie on the 3rd of April 2004. As I previously mentioned, I was a bridesmaid, and it is still one of the proudest days of my life. To see someone who had loved and lost before still believe in love, and still believe in happiness, made my heart swell. Here were two people ready to love and trust again and ready to put that faith in each other. The love on display that day was like nothing I had ever experienced. The room was full of love, and we had so much fun.

Dad was first married at a young age to a lady named Jane. It was a small ceremony with just him, Jane and two witnesses, which is about all I know. Dad never talked about his first wife, and the only story I have is that she left him while he was away at sea and took everything. Then he met my mother and married her on the 28th of January 1984, taking on a fatherly role to her three boys before I came along later the same year. My little brother, Nic, came along two years later. Mum and Dad were married for about 14 years before things broke down and they separated, divorcing in 2000. I recall many nights lying in bed, listening to their arguments, and my heart aches for children who go through this. It's important to know that marriages fail, and often it's no one's fault. It is never the children's fault.

CHAPTER TWELVE

Dad refused to give up on love, and when he met Julie, he was all in. He loved her humour, her compassion and her heart, and it was not long before the whole family fell in love with Julie and her family, too. To see Dad pick himself up from so many deemed failures inspired me to always find the learning in my failures and keep going.

Even on Dad's honeymoon after marrying Julie, he had a setback. Julie's passport was still in her maiden name, but they had booked the honeymoon in her married name. It was not until they had gotten through customs and were boarding the plane that the flight attendant realised the name difference, and they could not board. It was too late to get one of us to rush out their marriage certificate to the airport. Dad and Julie just laughed it off and flew out the following day. I always double check names on tickets and passports now thanks to this event!

Failure is a natural part of living. We all go through it. Sometimes it will be big, and sometimes it will be minor. But that day when I sat on the summit of Bluff Knoll and chatted away with Dad's angel, I realised that it's what we learn from our failures that is most important. It took me 12 months to be able to talk about my amazing achievement of hiking 350km alone and self-supported rather than talk about my failure of not reaching my goal of 1000km. I learnt that listening to your body (and sometimes your husband telling you to stop) is important and that we need to celebrate the achievement instead of focus on the failure. I learnt so much about myself on that hike – resilience, compassion, empathy, blister management – but most of all, I learnt to be kinder to myself.

Dad can rest assured that he never failed as a father because of what he taught me.

Thank you, Dad. Thank you for teaching me that it's how many times you get back up rather than how many times you fall that's important. Thank you for teaching me to learn from my failures, to take something with me into the future and grow from setbacks. Thank you for teaching me that sometimes, the lesson is actually in the failure.

CHAPTER THIRTEEN

It's OK to talk about it

"Communicate, even when it's uncomfortable or uneasy."
– Unknown

I grew up in a world of boys. I learnt from a young age that boys don't cry, and girls who do cry are emotional and "sissies". Basically, I learnt to keep my true feelings hidden and only show positive, happy emotions. I also learnt to stop complaining because I was incredibly lucky to have what I did. I don't particularly blame anyone for me growing up this way. It was just the way of the world. Even at school, it wasn't acceptable for boys to cry. And since I was a Navy brat, I also carried the stigma that anyone in the military must be incredibly tough.

When I was about 11, I went to hospital because I had an ingrown toenail. It was so bad, the doctor wanted to put me under anaesthetic so he could cut the toe open to remove the nail. I was in hospital overnight, and when I was discharged,

CHAPTER THIRTEEN

I relished all the attention I got. I was on crutches for a few days and was having fun with them when Mum took them off me and told me to toughen up because it was just a toenail. A few days later, when I went back to the doctor, we realised I had about 19 sutures in the toe, and the doctor was horrified that Mum had taken my crutches from me. Examples like this show how I was taught to believe that being "tough" was so important.

The Navy boys never talked about their feelings. I wish Dad had talked about his lost mates more. He often joked about his medals, particularly the one for special operations, but he never told me how hard it was, or how much things hurt. When I joined the police, I realised that this need to hide one's feelings was common in that workforce, too. You could be dealing with death, injury or horrible domestic violence situations at work. Then you and your colleagues might unwind at the pub afterwards and have a few beers, but no one would talk about how they felt or whether they were coping. The night I experienced my first fatality at work, I went home at 7am after a long night shift, poured myself a very big glass of red wine, sat on the couch with a huge plate of leftover lasagne, and ate and drank until I was numb. Another time, I emptied an entire canister of whipped cream into my mouth while lying on the couch, trying to process a shift where I had just discovered a 14-year-old girl prostituting herself on the streets.

Dad had his prostate operation in 2008; then things went downhill rapidly. This was surprising. Although we knew he was scared about the operation and worried he might not survive it, the prognosis post-op was great. The prostate was removed, and the doctors told us Dad would make a good recovery. However, Dad's mental health quickly deteriorated. He went from working full time in a busy job, where he was very much needed and respected, to suddenly sitting at home alone. Being alone with the odd beer throughout the day caused all the memories and emotions he had squashed down somewhere in the back of his mind to resurface. It wasn't long before Dad was having nightmares and struggled to get through a day without alcohol. He developed alcoholic dementia and forgot day-to-day things, such as turning off the stove. He would get on the roof to do something and not be able to get back down. I have a huge amount of respect for Julie and her work caring for Dad because it was definitely not an easy role.

I look back at this time in my life and kick myself for never talking to Dad about how he was feeling. I often asked him how he was physically, and lectured him about seeing a psychologist, which he eventually did and was diagnosed with PTSD from his early Navy days. However, I never sat down and said, "Dad, talk to me." We would tell jokes and stories and share memories, but he never opened up about his emotions, and I will forever regret that I didn't pry him open. I would get angry at him for drinking so much when I knew his liver was failing, but I never asked him why he was drinking. One day, I was so angry about the damage he was doing to his liver that I refused to talk to him until he stopped drinking. Two days later, a single red rose in a black box was delivered to me at work. The receptionist brought it to my desk and I read the note. It was from Dad, and it told me how much he loved me. My boss, who sat next to me, asked me if I was OK and I nodded, fighting back

CHAPTER THIRTEEN

the tears. When I called Dad to say thank you, I felt like a failure because I had broken my vow to not talk to him, yet I still didn't explain why I was being harsh. I thought that if he stopped drinking, he would be fine. I had no idea the drinking was his way of coping, and perhaps I should have listened instead of ignoring both our emotions, which continued to bubble away under the surface.

I avoided talking to anyone about Dad's health, and I am still not sure if I was in denial or reverting to my usual "hide the emotions" self. One day, I was caring for Dad at home so Julie could go out. He was incontinent by this stage and wearing adult diapers. Dad had an accident in the bathroom and was trying to clean it up when I walked into the laundry and realised what had happened. He had also fallen over. I helped Dad up and he told me to get out because he wanted to clean up the mess on the floor. I went to the living room and let him clean it up by himself, knowing he felt humiliated. I held in the emotion of seeing my big, strong Dad so helpless. I held my breath in the front room so I did not cry, and as soon as I could get out of that place, I did. I bawled my eyes out all the way home because I was embarrassed for Dad, but I was also ashamed that I couldn't deal with this and I couldn't just talk to him about it and let him know that it was OK, that I was there for him no matter what happened.

When Dad died, I didn't talk about it. I cried with my man that night, and then super strong Jaqui came out to play. I was strong for the family, I was strong at the funeral, and I had everything under control. Or so I thought. A week after the funeral, I went on a pre-planned trip to Melbourne.

I was meeting a girlfriend for the weekend while Jarrad had a boys' weekend at the races, and we would re-group on the Monday with all the partners ready for Melbourne Cup Day. This meant I would fly on my own rather than with Jarrad, and as soon as I was by myself, it hit me. The emotion came out in one big, horrible wave, and I could not control it. I was blessed to have a beautiful friend with me in Melbourne who just let me cry. I eventually met back up with Jarrad and started to talk to my man and best mate, and realised it was OK to talk about my feelings. They weren't judging me for being emotional. It was OK.

I remember being at my grandad's funeral at the age of 12, seeing Dad so strong and in control. I knew I wanted to be like that when I grew up. I am like that; however, I wish so much that I had given Dad a hug that day and asked him to tell me how he felt. I remember Dad losing a mate and instead of asking him about his friend, I tried to cheer him up with jokes and pranks and we watched comedy movies. This was a common theme in our relationship and something I find myself still reverting to today. I want to make someone feel better, so instead of sitting with them in their sadness or grief, I crack inappropriate jokes and try to make them laugh. I wish that I had instead asked Dad how he was feeling.

Not long after his surgery, Dad was still attached to a catheter when he had a family court date for a matter that was ongoing after about five years. My mother was still trying to sue him for child support, despite all the evidence showing Dad had paid over and above. We thought the matter was going to be finalised in court that day and we were looking

CHAPTER THIRTEEN

forward to it being resolved. I think we had even put a bottle of Champagne in the fridge to celebrate when we got home. However, the magistrate said that Mum had asked for more time, and so it was granted. Dad stood up on shaking legs and read a pre-scripted letter to the magistrate, explaining the mental toll this court process was taking on him. It took all my strength to sit behind him in that courtroom and see his legs shaking and hear his voice trembling while he pleaded for relief from the magistrate. We walked out of the courtroom in silence, emotionally drained and upset that it was not all over. Again, I said nothing on the way home, and after dropping Dad off, I cried all the way home. I even had to stay home from work that night because I couldn't stop the tears. Why didn't I just cry with Dad?

After Dad's death, I was really interested in how the mind worked, particularly with his PTSD and coping mechanisms. So, I enrolled in university remotely to study psychology. At the time, I was unsure how much of the course I would complete, and I told myself I would take it one unit at a time. But I was fascinated by the content and fell in love with learning again. I was working full time, training for my ultramarathons, and would spend my nights and weekends reading textbooks. I learnt to record my notes and listen to them on my long training runs. I wanted to understand why we feel the need to be "strong" and put on a brave face all the time rather than open up to our emotions and talk about how we truly feel. I wanted to be able to open up more and talk about my feelings, and I wanted to encourage this in my family and friends. It took me six years to complete the course, and I felt Dad with me as I walked out on stage to get my degree. I was incredibly proud of the work I had done, but even more, I was so grateful to be able to change my own beliefs and thoughts later in my life. I now lead a life of curiosity and want to always learn more because of the journey this degree took me on.

I will never get the time back with Dad to ask questions about how he felt or what made him emotional, but I have learnt from this. I have learnt that it's OK for boys to cry, it's OK for anyone to talk about how they feel, and I encourage it. I can now talk about my emotions without fear of shame or judgement, and I encourage everyone to do so. As I witnessed with Dad, your health will suffer if you do not talk about it.

Thank you, Dad. You probably didn't realise it, but our inability to talk about our emotions at the time has made me grow into a stronger woman. I am more vulnerable, open and honest. Thank you for giving me the inspiration to share my emotions and use your story to help others learn the importance of being open. Thank you for making me understand it is OK to talk about it. I'm sorry we did not learn this lesson earlier.

CHAPTER FOURTEEN

Festina lente

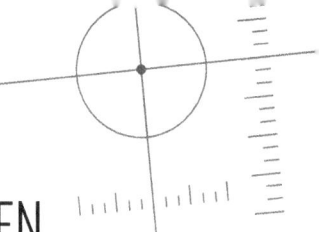

"Hasten slowly and ye shall soon arrive."
– Milarepa

I have a motto in life: *Festina lente*. Most people have no idea what this means, but it means something to me.

My life can get very chaotic at times. I love to achieve, so I am great at taking on more and more and then realising I'm spiralling into a world of all work and no play, and self-care goes out the window. So, it is fitting that *Festina lente* means "hasten slowly".

Of the submarines he served on, Dad's favourite was HMAS *Onslow*, one of six Oberon class submarines in the Royal Australian Navy. He loved the crew and made lifelong mates on some of their deployments. Dad first served on *Onslow* on the 13th of June 1977 and was with her until March 1981, when he was deployed to the submarine support base at HMAS *Platypus* in Sydney. There, he worked as the engineering and weapons workshop supervisor. On board *Onslow*, Dad was well known for organising social and sporting activities for both the engineering department and

CHAPTER FOURTEEN

the ship's company. After *Platypus*, he returned to *Onslow* in 1982 as the deputy marine engineering officer until he injured his back in October 1985.

I was born while Dad was serving on *Onslow*. Two months after my birth, he arranged to have my christening on board. Of course, I do not remember my christening, but I love looking back at the photos of Dad in his Navy dress whites and my godparents in the control room of the submarine. Every ship and boat in the Navy has a bell that hangs on the front of the deck. The Navy chaplain turned this bell upside down, put the holy water in it, and used it to christen me. My full name was then engraved inside the rim of the bell. It is incredibly special, and telling people I was christened on board a submarine is a great icebreaker. The boat was decommissioned in 1999 and proudly sits in Sydney Harbour as part of the Australian National Maritime Museum. When I travel to Sydney for work, which is often, I love to run past *Onslow* and whisper a prayer to Dad. Since the sub's decommissioning, the bell now sits at the Australian War Museum in Canberra, and I look forward to visiting it soon to show my husband.

When I was about 12 years old, my bedroom was down the end of the hallway in our house. The hallway was lined with pictures of insignia from the boats that Dad had served on. If I lay in my bed with my bedroom door open, I could see the *Onslow* insignia on the wall: a judge's white wig with a small map below it and the words, *Festina lente*, underneath. Dad explained that the judge's wig represented Sir Alexander Onslow and the submarine was named after the town of Onslow, in northern WA. Sir Onslow was the third chief justice of the supreme court of Western Australia.

The words *Festina lente*, Dad said, meant "hasten slowly". At the young age of 12, I didn't understand what that meant, but Dad explained that when I am in a hurry to get something done, *Festina lente* meant to get it done but slow down a little to make sure you get it right. Too often, we rush into things too fast and put ourselves in danger. This didn't mean a huge amount to a 12-year-old, but as I have grown, I have used this line on many occasions to remind myself to stop and think about things before rushing in, but also not to overthink them and avoid taking action altogether. Hasten – but think about it first!

This boat was a huge part of Dad's life. In 2009, a story surfaced about a sailor on board who had died from carbon monoxide poisoning. On the 1st of March 1981, *Onslow* was participating in war games off the coast of Australia and stopped "snorting" (this is when air is taken and expelled through a snorkel). The snorkel was somehow sealed, and carbon monoxide flooded the submarine. One crew member was killed, and another 18 were rendered unconscious. A third of the crew was found to have absorbed twice the lethal limit of carbon monoxide into their blood. Although it happened in 1981, it was kept classified until 2009. I don't know much about the story other than what the media reported. There was a Sunday night segment about it on TV and I remember watching it with Dad, and he was crying. It wasn't until many years later, after his death, when I had his service records that I understood that Dad was on board that day.

CHAPTER FOURTEEN

The media highlighted the fact that all the sailors on board were not provided with any psychological counselling after the incident. They were given one week off, and because the incident was classified, everyone had to keep quiet about it. It's another moment where I wish I had asked Dad more questions about it to understand what he had gone through and how he was feeling. And it's another reminder that it's OK to talk about it and seek help when you're emotionally struggling. Dad only stayed on board *Onslow* until the end of March 1981 before going back to HMAS *Platypus*, which was at the submarine depot based in Neutral Bay, Sydney. He didn't return to HMAS *Onslow* until June 1982.

Onslow had an interesting life. She was commissioned on the 26th of December 1969 and arrived in Sydney in July 1970. She had a few scary incidents, including one in 1972 when she dived to 1,201 feet – much deeper than the operating depth of 660 feet. A ballast tank overfilled with water and forced her into a steep dive crash. The boat and the men on board were lucky to survive. Dad was on board HMAS *Onslow* when she had a hugely successful exercise against the United States Navy in 1980, ending with the crew hoisting a Jolly Roger flag from their communication mast to celebrate their success.

Dad took me to Sydney Harbour in 1999 to see HMAS *Onslow* decommissioned. It was one of the most valued trips I ever had with Dad. The two of us headed to Sydney to stay with his very good friend and my treasured Aunty Kate. We spent about four days sightseeing and catching up with old friends, which was the best time for me. It's the only memory I have of Dad and I having a holiday together alone, and it's such a dear memory. I gained a better understanding of Dad's Navy life and met some of his old friends, who told a few stories about Dad having cocktail parties on submarines and being a larrikin. Despite many stories of fun and adventure, Dad's mates made it clear to me that they respected Dad as a "Chief Tiff" (chief petty officer), and they trusted him with their lives. I had quality time with my Aunty Kate, who I still catch up with. Despite not being a blood aunty, I draw a lot of inspiration from her. She lived a life of adventure and worked hard on her own business before she retired. She isn't married, and I looked up to her as a female role model for her independence and strength when I was a young girl. I still do.

When we went on board HMAS *Onslow*, we didn't need a tour guide because Dad had served on her, so we could go about as we pleased. Our photo was taken in the same spot where Dad held me on my christening day, and I still treasure both these photos. As we neared the end of the sub, we passed the torpedo tubes, where a tour guide was telling tourists about the torpedoes and how they worked. One guy thought he would be funny and asked how many cartons of duty-free beer could fit in a torpedo tube. The tour guide laughed, and Dad chimed in and said, "One hundred and eight. The last eight you need to hold in the door as you shut it." It became evident very quickly that Dad had served on the boat, and just like that, he became the tour guide. The group loved hearing his stories about "snorting backwards through the Dardanelles". He certainly embellished some of the stories, but the tourists lapped it up, and some had their photo taken with him. I was such a proud daughter, standing back and watching these people enjoy Dad's stories. Dad

CHAPTER FOURTEEN

had been known as the "Beer Bosun" on board *Onslow* and oversaw beer safety and distribution. One of my favourite stories was about the submarine firing a water shot, sending all the duty-free beer into the ocean, and making many grown men sob! Dad wasn't on board for this event, but he loved to relay the story. He had such a gift when it came to storytelling, and I loved to listen and laugh, even when I knew he was stretching the truth a little for the sake of an entertaining story. Dad loved the motto of the Australian Submarines, "stealth and strength", and his favourite line was "DBF", which meant "diesel boats forever". He loved to share this with the American sailors, who preferred their big nuclear submarines to our little diesel subs. It was also a favourite line when the Aussies beat the Americans in their war games.

Not long after this holiday, I received a gift from Dad. It was a small plaque sitting on a stand that read, "First a daughter, now a friend."

Thank you, Dad. Thank you for teaching me the importance of *Festina lente*. Thank you for giving me a motto I have taken into my life and created success with. Thank you for sharing your Navy stories with me, especially the hard ones. Thank you for serving our beautiful country and teaching me the importance of respecting those who have.

CHAPTER FIFTEEN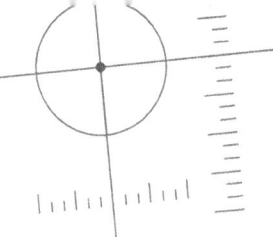

Saying goodbye

"If ever there is tomorrow when we're not together… there is something you must always remember. You are braver than you believe, stronger than you seem, and smarter than you think. But the most important thing is, even if we're apart… I'll always be with you."
– Winnie the Pooh

Everyone feels and reacts differently when someone they love dies. Some people curl up and go into hibernation, some go into shock, and some get busy. Everyone has their own way of dealing with grief. I can still recall the day of Dad's death and feel the emotion as if it were yesterday. I am incredibly grateful for my husband and his strong arms that wrapped me in his love.

The day after Dad's death, I felt very hungover and tired. I travelled to the funeral home to meet Nic and Julie, and we all felt rather similar. The funeral home was near one of our favourite pubs, so we promised each other we would get through the next half an hour and then have parmas for lunch! I have attended more funerals than I can count, but it is vastly different having to arrange a funeral for someone

CHAPTER FIFTEEN

you love. How do you even give the perfect send off? Humour was my way of dealing with grief, and it turned out Nic and Julie were the same. I am not sure how the funeral director put up with us, cracking jokes, not knowing all the family names, and asking if we could use a cardboard box for the cremation rather than a coffin because it was cheaper! We made jokes whenever we could because we knew it was how we could cope. I will never forget the feeling that came over me as I walked into the room full of empty coffins, and we were told to "choose" one. My body tingled all over, and I felt the urge to run. I felt so overwhelmed that this was even happening. After about three hours, we walked out of the funeral home tired, hungry and emotional. We walked straight into the pub for beers and parmas all round and started responding to all the messages asking for the funeral date.

This was the moment I clicked into action mode. I felt it like a switch. I was on the phone to various aunties, uncles and friends, and got everyone organised. The funeral was in four days, so we had a lot to do in a short timeframe. Within a few days, we had arranged beds for all the interstate and international guests, we had organised the wake, and we had confirmed the ceremony. The people who stepped up and helped us were amazing; from food at the wake, to driving my family to the funeral, to just supporting us. It was an incredible display of love and respect, and Dad would have been proud of them all.

Dad's funeral was everything I had hoped he would want, and I believe it was the perfect send off. Family flew in from around the world. In the days leading up to it, I was back and forth between home and the airport to pick up aunts, uncles and cousins who came to stay. I was so grateful for our big house. Two aunts shared the spare bed, one uncle slept on the floor, and a cousin was in the theatre room. This extended to another four bodies crashing on the floor on the night of the funeral! It was a home full of love, and I wouldn't have had it any other way.

There was standing room only at Dad's funeral, and even that was limited. Dad had the ugliest jumper in the world that his mother had knitted for him when he was a teenager. He called it Fred, and he loved that jumper so much. The jumper's arms were very wide, almost like the bottom of a pair of flares from the '70s. When Dad went to the cricket in his younger days, the arms of the jumper were so long that he could hold a six-pack of beer cans in each hand, slip them up the jumper sleeve, and no one would know a thing! I had often worn the jumper for fancy dress parties, especially anything '70s or '80s themed, and I am certain it had never been washed. Julie offered to give the jumper to Dad's big sister; however, Penny took one look, and potentially one smell, of Fred, and decided it was better that Fred continued to keep Dad warm. We all agreed that Fred could go in the coffin with him. When we asked the funeral director if we could put Fred in the coffin with Dad, his face changed into one of pure shock. It was hilarious! We quickly realised that we needed to explain that Fred was a jumper. It was good to start the morning with a laugh.

As everyone arrived for the service, some family and I snuck into the room to say our final goodbyes with the coffin open. My aunt stuffed Fred into the coffin with Dad and gave her

CHAPTER FIFTEEN

brother one last kiss. Dad looked so peaceful and relaxed, wearing his best suit, and I am sure he even had a smile on his face. My heart was full knowing he was no longer in pain. My brothers walked Dad's coffin to the front of the room, surrounded by sailors in their smart white uniforms giving Dad a guard of honour. He was draped in a white ensign flag that the Navy had permitted us to use, and rosemary was laid across his coffin. The eulogy was delivered by Dad's mate, Peter, his big sister, Penny, Julie, and me. I recall standing at the front of the room to talk to everyone and being so blown away by the love and support in that room. Men in white uniforms and men I had grown up calling uncle laid bare their emotions, and it made me so proud of Dad for the life he had lived. I had thought that giving his eulogy would be one of the hardest moments of my life. Instead, it was one of the proudest. I was so proud to be up there as his daughter, talking about his amazing life.

My eulogy for Dad read:

> *I don't need to tell you all Dad's life stories. He did a great job of making sure everyone heard his stories – usually more than once. Instead, I am going to speak from the heart.*
>
> *Dad may have been young in his death, but he lived a full life worthy of a huge send off. Every life has its ups and downs, and while Dad's had plenty of downs, he was always ready to celebrate the ups in life and taught me to appreciate good times with friends and family.*
>
> *I want to celebrate the ups in Dad's life today. The birth of his children, becoming an uncle, marrying Julie, seeing his*

stepchildren marry and becoming Poppy Pete to their kids. He never shied at telling us how proud he was of everything we did, but also telling everyone else as well! He was stepfather to Noel, Dean and Mark before fathering myself and then Nicholas. He then took on April and Ed when he married Julie, and was also uncle to Charlotte, James and Richard, and Poppy Pete to Cameron, Aussie and Lucas, and only three days before his death, twins Thomas and Christopher were born. He also welcomed everyone, including Julie's beautiful family, into his life with open arms. I honestly believe that his life was so full that April had to recently give birth to twins because one life coming into this world wasn't going to be enough to make up for Dad leaving this world.

Dad was the strongest man I have ever known. From his Navy days as Chief Tiff on the O-boats to personal tragedies, he always showed his strength and made sure his friends and family were cared for and loved. Most people here today would agree that he would open the door to anyone if they needed a feed, a beer or a couch to crash on.

Dad loved his cricket, trains, subs and Lee Marvin movies. But more than anything, he loved his friends and family, and he would be so happy to know you are all here not only to say goodbye but also to ensure he goes out in style. Thank you all so much for being here today and helping make that possible. Thank you also to everyone who has assisted Julie and I the past few years in ensuring that Dad had a great quality of life right to the very end.

Dad never let the truth get in the way of a good story, especially when the garbage truck was involved. He could

CHAPTER FIFTEEN

sit and tell us stories forever, and he has probably already started telling them in heaven. From his submarine tales to bragging about his family or telling everyone they were the ugliest man he had ever met (something he often told my other half), he could entertain you for hours or drive you crazy!

Dad was always supportive of anything I wanted to do, telling me never to wait for my ship to come in but to swim out and meet it. He taught me to drive, he taught me to appreciate red wine, and he taught me to work hard and party hard. I was 17 when I moved in with Dad in his little flat in Rocki, and we lived together for a while. It was a magical time for both of us, especially when little brother Nic came to stay and the three of us would eat spag bog, drink red wine and watch movies after spending the day on the beach at Garden Island together. I loved the three of us together and will never forget those good times we shared.

One day, Dad met his perfect match in Julie, and I am so glad he got to experience the joy and happiness that came with being married to her. I was so proud to stand alongside them when they exchanged their vows. Julie brought April and Ed along with her, and the family gatherings were bigger and noisier but happier for having them. I will forever be in debt to Julie for the love and care she has provided to Nic and I, but more importantly, to Dad, who loved you so very much. Julie and I were with him at the end, and we will forever share that special bond.

Recently, I spent the weekend with Dad for Father's Day, and the power went out at night for five hours. So, there we were, eating fish and chips in the dark with candles, and we reflected on a lot of things we have done together, a lot of things we accomplished together, and Dad told me that while I will always be his daughter, he was so proud to call me a friend as well. I will carry that night with me forever.

I am proud of Dad for the man he was, but also for making me the person I am today. My strength is from him, my running is for him, my humour is from him, but thank god my nose is not! While I will walk my own path, he has helped pave the way for me, and I will forever be grateful for his love and guidance.

As the service finished, "The Last Post" rang out with the eerie sound of the bugle, and we moved on to toast Dad at the local RSL club.

I was swept along in the magic of the ex-submariners at the RSL club. They hugged me, laughed with me, told me stories, fed me sandwiches, and we toasted all afternoon with the finest Scotch. It was a beautiful afternoon and a fitting goodbye. We all piled into a few cars afterwards, and most of us ended up back at my place, where we continued to toast and tell stories well into the night. I woke the following morning to find one brother and his family sleeping on the floor of my study, and another brother sleeping in his swag on the tray of his ute in my driveway. Along with all the family already staying at my place, I could not have been more surrounded by love.

Dad's ashes were handed over to the Navy to distribute into the ocean. We didn't know when or how it would be done,

CHAPTER FIFTEEN

but the Navy knew what Dad's wishes were, so we left it with them. We had said our goodbye the way we had wanted, and Julie and I were confident Dad would have loved his send off. A while later, Julie received a call from one of Dad's mates in the Navy, who had arranged the opportunity for Julie and two others to be present while Dad's ashes were spread. Julie asked Nic and me if we wanted to attend. We were so humbled to be invited to share this moment. The whole thing was a secret because of security concerns, and even we didn't know what to expect, with our only briefing to wear good shoes. We met Dad's mate in Fremantle, where we were put on board a small dinghy and taken out to a submarine anchored off the coast. We then climbed up a rope ladder onto the sub's deck and were greeted by the captain and his crew, all dressed in their Navy dress whites. My breath was taken away as I climbed onto the deck and saw all these sailors dressed up and ready to greet us. It was a warm but overcast day – "good submarine weather", we were told. The rain threatened us from afar but never made an appearance. The sea remained calm, and the smell of the ocean and the sound of it slapping against the side of the submarine was comforting and beautiful. It felt so incredibly peaceful.

The captain knew Dad from his time as a junior. Dad had signed his performance review, which saw him receive his dolphins badge and become a submariner. I loved this personal story as the captain performed a small ceremony to farewell Dad. Another sailor and his wife were also being farewelled, and we joined their three representatives to say goodbye. The ashes were in a small canister, and the crew had set up a long tube that ran from the deck to the water's edge to avoid the ashes blowing away. When a submarine is on the surface, the deck is a few metres above sea level. The captain blew his whistle and poured the ashes down the tube into the water. He then threw a set of submariner's "dolphins" into the ashes. The splash as they hit the water and then the silence as they sank into the sea took my breath away again. It was incredibly powerful, and the magic of this moment was like nothing I had ever experienced. Not only was I experiencing the emotion of saying goodbye again to Dad, but I was also so happy that he got his perfect send off. This was exactly how he wanted his ashes to be spread and exactly how I wanted to remember him – at one with the sea. I was asked to read something at the ceremony, and I chose one of Dad's favourite poems:

"I Must Go Down To The Sea Again" by Spike Milligan

I must go down to the sea again,
To the lonely sea and the sky;
I left my shoes and socks there –
I wonder if they're dry?

It was very typical of Dad's humour, and I could almost feel him chuckling at it.

Now, many years later, I often visit the ocean to talk to Dad. It doesn't matter which ocean or where in the world I am, I can feel his presence, and I can tell him anything. I feel Dad around me on many occasions. When a door slams while I am talking about him, I tell myself it's him listening. When the wind blows feathers across my path while I am running and mulling over a difficult decision, I feel him there.

CHAPTER FIFTEEN

When Jarrad and I moved to Melbourne, we boarded our one-way flight and were seated in row 53 – Dad's number.

There is so much Dad taught me, and I only hope I have done it justice with our story. On occasion, I find myself telling a story and realise that I sound just like him. My inner storyteller comes out, and I know I got that from him. I will continue to go on telling stories, just like him.

Thank you, Dad.

"The Submariner's Prayer"

O Father, hear our prayer to thee
From your humble servants
Beneath the sea.

In the depths of oceans, as oft we stray,
So far from night, so far from day,
We would ask your guiding light to glow,
To make our journey safe below.

Please oft times grant us patient mind,
Then 'ere the darkness won't us blind.
We seek thy protection from the deep,
And grant us peace when 'ere we sleep.

Of our homes and loved ones far away,
We ask you care for them each day
Until we surface once again
To drink the air and feel the rain.

We ask your guiding hand to show
A safe progression sure and slow.
Dear Lord, please hear our prayer to thee,
From your humble servants
Beneath the sea.

Amen

www.ingramcontent.com/pod-product-compliance
Lightning Source LLC
Chambersburg PA
CBHW070811100426
42742CB00012B/2331